CourseBook Series

The CourseBook Series is the product of Dr. Mark H. Kavanaugh. Dr. Kavanaugh is a Professor of Psychology and Social Sciences at Kennebec Valley Community College. The CourseBooks contain the teaching content for each course.

Format

While definitively designed for digital distribution, each CourseBook is available in a number of formats. Distribution of the multi-touch ebook version is done exclusively through Apple Books. These CourseBooks may be purchased and downloaded directly to any iOS or Mac device.

Print versions of the CourseBooks are also available and are distributed through Amazon Kindle Unlimited.

Editing and Errors

Dr. Kavanaugh has written and edited all of this material but he is a horrible editor. He also cannot afford to have the work professionally reviewed. Mistakes, misspellings, broken links, and other errors may exist. Readers are encouraged to contact Dr. Kavanaugh directly to inform him of these errors for the next edition!

Copyright and Use

Dr. Kavanaugh owns the rights to the entire CourseBook. Others are free to use the CourseBook without permission. Graphics within the CourseBook are the original creations of Dr. Kavanaugh, downloaded from his Adobe Stock account, or are accompanied by attribution.

Index

How this CourseBook Works

The content of this CourseBook aligns with activities, expectations, and assignments that are found in the KVCC Learning Management System (LMS).

Students are expected to read and absorb the information in the CourseBook, read and review any textbook or other reading assignments, review the Assessment expectations outlined in each CourseBook Chapter, and participate in the expectations set by the instructor of the course in the LMS.

Chapter Organization

Each Chapter has been organized using an instructional design model called ALOTA, provides an outline of course materials that adheres to long-standing instructional design theory for adult learners. Namely, the model is greatly influenced by Gagne's Nine Events of Instruction

ALOTA

ALOTA is an acronym for the four essential parts of a lesson plan (or, in this case, chapter):

Attention

Learning Outcomes

Teaching

Assessment

Each Chapter in the CourseBooks series is organized in this manner in order to guide students through the material they are expected to learn.

Attention

Images, videos, text, and/or activities that bring readers into the focus of the lesson.

Learning Outcomes

Adhering to the language of Blooms Taxonomy of Learning Objectives, this section outlines the performance-based learning outcomes for the lesson. These align with the Assessment section of each lesson.

Teaching

This section can contain any variety of resources including text, lectures, recordings, videos, and links that provide a pathway through material to assist students in readying themselves for the Assessments.

Assessments

This section outlines assignments for students to demonstrate learning.

Additional Resources

Dr. K's Psychobabble

Dr. Kavanaugh also maintains a YouTube Channel called Dr. K's Psychobabble. You may find some of these videos embedded within this CourseBook.

Visit Dr. K's Psychobabble YouTube Channel

QR Codes

In order to ensure that readers of the print version of this CourseBook can still access online content, I have included QR Codes (such as the one listed here under my icon for Dr. K's Psychobabble.

Most smart phones are able to scan these codes with their camera and access the online material!

Apps in the CourseBook

Occasionally I will find mobile applications that relate to course content or are simply fun and engaging ways to learn. I will include links to these apps as the appear in the Apple App Store. It is likely that the same app is also available in Google Play but I will not usually provide the direct link to Google Play in the CourseBook.

Outcomes Alignment

Alignment With the Guidelines From the American Psychological Association

The American Psychological Association (APA) produces guidelines for the development of curriculum in the teaching of Psychology at the undergraduate level.

Here is a direct link to the document

The CourseBook series is designed to outline instructional materials and activities for demonstrating competence and knowledge in Psychology in alignment with these guidelines.

This section of each Psychology CourseBook will outline the specific content and activities (assessments) that align with the APA expectations.

Knowledge Base in Psychology

Describe key concepts, principles, and over-arching themes in psychology.

- N/A

Develop a working knowledge of psychology's content domains.

- Chapter 5 Discussion - Statistics
- Chapter 9 Discussion - Outcomes

Describe applications of Psychology.

- Chapter 3 Assignment - Plan
- Chapter 8 Discussion A - Chance

- Chapter 10 Assignment - Self

Scientific Inquiry and Critical Thinking

Use scientific reasoning to interpret psychological phenomena.

- N/A

Demonstrate psychology information literacy.

- Chapter 5 Discussion - Statistics

Engage in innovative and integrative thinking and problem solving.

- Chapter 6 Discussion - Bias

Interpret, design, and conduct basic psychological research.

- N/A

Incorporate sociocultural factors in scientific inquiry.

- N/A

Ethical and Social Responsibility in a Diverse World

Apply ethical standards to evaluate psychological science and practice.

- N/A

Build and enhance interpersonal relationships.

- Chapter 7 Assignment - Planning

Adopt values that build community at local, national, and global levels.

- N/A

Communication

Demonstrate effective writing for different purposes.

- Chapter 5 Quiz - APA Reference
- Chapter 5 Assignment - Article

Exhibit effective presentation skills for different purposes.

- N/A

Interact effectively with others.

- Chapter 2 Assignment - Advising
- Chapter 7 Assignment - Planning
- Chapter 10 Discussion - Class

Professional Development

Apply psychological content and skills to career goals.

- Chapter 2 Discussion - KVCC PSY
- Chapter 7 Assignment - Planning
- Chapter 8 Discussion B - Career
- Chapter 10 Assignment - Self

Exhibit self-efficacy and self-regulation.

- Chapter 6 Quiz - Scavenger Hunt
- Chapter 10 Discussion - Class
- Chapter 10 Assignment - Self

Refine project management skills.

- Chapter 3 Assignment - Plan

Enhance teamwork capacity.

- Chapter 2 Assignment - Advising

Develop meaningful professional direction for life after graduation.

- Chapter 8 Discussion B - Career

Alignment with the Essential Learning Outcomes of Kennebec Valley Community College and with the AAC&U VALUE Rubrics

In addition to the Learning Outcomes associated with the APA, specific to the field of Psychology, Kennebec Valley Community College has adopted a set of "Essential Learning Outcomes" (ELOs) which operationalize the institutional goal of producing an "Educated Person" upon graduation.

These Learning Outcomes are largely based upon the VALUE Rubrics produced by the Association of American Colleges & Universities (AAC&U).

This particular program goes further than the expectations of KVCC's ELOs and incorporates content and activities (assessments) and address all of the VALUE Rubrics.

KVCC's Essential Learning Outcomes

The following section outlines the areas in this Course-Book that address specific ELO competencies.

Critical Thinking

- Chapter 3 Discussion - Time
- Chapter 6 Discussion - Bias

Interpersonal Communication

- Chapter 2 Assignment - Advising

Oral Communication

- N/A

Problem Solving

- Chapter 3 Discussion - Time
- Chapter 3 Assignment - Plan
- Chapter 6 Quiz - Scavenger Hunt
- Chapter 7 Assignment - Planning

- Chapter 8 Discussion B - Career

Quantitative Literacy

- Chapter 5 Discussion - Statistics

Teamwork

- Chapter 2 Assignment - Advising

Written Communication

- Chapter 5 Quiz - APA Reference
- Chapter 5 Assignment - Article

AAC&U VALUE Rubrics (not included in the list above)

The following section outlines the areas in this Course-Book that address specific VALUE competencies.

Civic Engagement

- N/A

Creative Thinking

- Chapter 8 Discussion A - Chance
- Chapter 10 Assignment - Self

Ethical Reasoning

- Chapter 6 Discussion - Bias

Foundational Skills for Lifelong Learning

- Chapter 8 Discussion A - Chance
- Chapter 8 Discussion B - Career

Global Learning

- N/A

Information Literacy

- Chapter 6 Discussion - Bias

Inquiry and Analysis

- Chapter 10 Assignment - Self

Integrative Learning

- Chapter 4 Discussion - My Tech

- Chapter 4 Assignment - ZOOM

- Chapter 8 Discussion B - Career

- Chapter 9 Discussion - Outcomes

Intercultural Knowledge

- Chapter 10 Discussion - Class

Reading

- Chapter 1 Discussion - Excitement

Psychology Seminar

This CourseBook was designed as an introduction to the Associates of Science in Psychology at Kennebec Valley Community College. It explores establishing a learning community, technology expertise, psychological information literacy, APA writing style, academic and career planning, and course/program/institutional assessment.

Changes made to this Edition of the CourseBook

1. This is the first edition.

About the Author

Mark H. Kavanaugh, Ph.D.

Mark Kavanaugh has been writing, teaching, and integrating technology into instruction for decades. He holds a Masters in Counseling, Masters in Instructional and Performance Technology, and a Ph.D. in Educational Psychology. Mark lives in Maine with his wife Katie.

Visit Mark's Website

Organization

1

Attention

Expectations

Even though many students and instructors are experienced at learning and teaching online, research has long supported the importance of clarifying both student and teacher expectations (Bozarth, Chapman, & LaMonica, 2004). Since so many courses utilize significant online tools, even if the course has face-to-face, interactions there is still a need to identify these expectations explicitly.

Different teachers will organize their course materials in different ways. In this course, you are going to be introduced to the way in which Mark Kavanaugh organizes most of the courses in the Department of Social Sciences and Psychology at Kennebec Valley Community College.

As the Chair of the Department (the manager) I take responsibility for the creation and structure of nearly every course under my supervision. They are structured and presented in the same way. Once you have mastered the way I design this class, the design and structure of all the courses in the Department will become more clear.

My methods are evidenced based. There is very little in the design of my classes that his not based on research on the art of teaching and learning, both online and face-to-face. I have taught over 350 college-level courses and over 180 of them have been completely online. Not only do I have lots of experience teaching, I also have educational credentials.

My initial educational journey earned me a BS in Psychology and an MS in Counseling. However, when I started teaching full-time, I earned an additional MS in Instructional and Performance Technology (the MOST useful degree I have!) and completed my Ph.D. in Educational Psychology with an emphasis on distance learning.

This does not mean that my methods always work and it does not mean they are perfect. I make modifications to what I do when I realize that things don't work and when my students inform me that things don't work!

I ALWAYS welcome your comments on my methods and I take constructive criticism very seriously.

At the same time…

I also have high expectations of my students. Learning is a two-way path that only comes about when I do the best work I can do and you, the student, does the best work you can do. I have seen students succeed in my classes, even with tremendous obstacles if they focus their energies on the following tips:

GO TO CLASS

While this may seem straight forward, students actually often skip class, or fail to log into their online classes on a regular (daily) basis. Communication about the material, study tips, and all the instruction of class takes place in the classroom. If you are NOT there you cannot benefit from these experiences. This is regardless of whether YOU feel the classes are worth attending or not.

- **Attend** scheduled class meetings.
- Log into your online course **every day**.
- **Pay attention** to your course Announcements and Discussions.
- Arrive at class with a well-rested, well-fed, and appropriately "motivated" to learn **state of mind**.

DO YOUR HOMEWORK

To be successful in class you will need to read stuff, take quizzes and tests, do presentations, write reports, etc. This is the "work" associated with going to school. You need to do ALL the assessments and activities for EVERY class. They are there to reinforce your learning and to inform the instructor and you as to how well you are acquiring the information.

- **Read** the course material.
- Read instructions very **carefully** and for **detail**.
- Complete the assignments **on time**.
- **Review the feedback** that your instructor provides on your performance regardless of the grade you got.

ASK QUESTIONS

You may have heard that there are no "stupid questions"...well, there are. I've encountered some of them and those are not the type of questions you need to ask. Here are some examples:

- Will skipping this test effect my grade?
- Can I use this textbook I already own instead of the one you want me to have?
- Are you going to be going over anything important in class today?

However, MOST questions are not like these at all...and you need to ask them!

You also need to make sure that you are asking the best person possible for the answer. Your instructor is usually the best person to ask about any aspect of the course. They are the ones that know this information best. Do not rely on others in the class for these kinds of questions.

Bozarth, J., Chapman, D.D., & LaMonica, L. (2004). Preparing for distance learning: Designing an online student orientation course. *Education Technology & Society, 7*(1), 87-106.

Learning Outcomes

Upon completion of this Chapter, students should be able to:

1. Identify course requirements within the syllabus.

2. Access course materials for offline use.

3. Identify the integration of web-based tools and the CourseBook.

4. Identify the utility of the Course Timeline.

5. Demonstrate the use of Discussions, Quizzes, and Assignments in the learning management system (LMS).

Teaching

Note on Teaching: This section will describe all the material that you ned to review to complete the Assessment section successfully. While this section is akin to a "Lecture" in class, not all the information you need to complete the assessments are contained in these pages. Other sources such as your textbook, Online resources, movies, etc. may need to be reviewed.

Welcome!

What an exciting time to be studying Psychology! This course is a form of extended orientation to the Associates of Science in Psychology at Kennebec Valley Community College. My hope is that this course will assist you in charting your path through the program and beyond. This is also a course that will enable you to determine if you are in the RIGHT program for you achieve your ultimate personal and academic goals.

Organization

In this first Chapter, you are going to learn about how the materials in this class are organized. This class, and. avast majority of the courses in the Department of Social Sciences and Psychology, was designed by Dr. Mark Kavanaugh. Once you understand and have mastered the organization of this class, you will find that most of the other social sciences classes are organized in the exact same way!

Major Tools

Let me summarize the major tools associated with all of these classes.

Learning Management System

A learning management system, or LMS, is an online tool specifically designed to use as a teaching tool. It allows instructors to organize and present information online. The online site allows students to interact with the course material, with their instructor and with their fellow students.

Many teachers use the LMS to post course materials, to deliver online quizzes and exams, and to provide a place for students to submit their work.

Kennebec Valley Community College has adopted an LMS that goes by the name of Brightspace.

Nearly every course at KVCC utilizes Brightspace in one way or another. For online classes (classes that do not have any face-to-face meetings), Brightspace is the virtual classroom.

When you log into Brightspace using your student log in credentials, you will see a list of the courses you are currently registered for that utilize Brightspace. Clicking on the names of these courses will bring you to that class' Brightspace site.

Organization

Although the general layout of a Brightspace course is standardized, different teachers organize the material in their Brightspace courses in different ways. In this class you will find just a few links in the site once you enter the class.

Overview/Syllabus

In this section you will find basic information about the course, a small video about navigating in BS, information about the CourseBook and any textbooks, information on contacting the instructor for the course, student support information, and a copy of the syllabus.

It is **vital** to read the entire syllabus of any course you are taking in order to understand the expectations of the course. The syllabus is presented so you can read it online, but you can also print the syllabus and use it as a guide to the course as you progress.

Course Timeline

The Course Timeline serves as the point of access to all the discussions, quizzes, and assignments in this class. It organizes these links in a timeline representing the progress through the material during the weeks of the class.

The Timeline serves as a calendar telling you when material will be covered and when assessments are due. The name of each assessment is actually a link to the discussion, quiz, or assignment drop box that you will use to participate in class and/or submit your work.

This document can also be printed and used as a guide through the class, but it is also a "living document". Your instructor can change the order of content and due dates on this page.

CourseBook

It seems a bit silly to introduce the concept of the CourseBook in the CourseBook itself. Clearly you have accessed this document!

The CourseBook is the core source of content for the class. Each Chapter corresponds to the Chapters listed in the Course Timeline. Each Chapter contains information that you must review in order to be successful ion the course.

You can learn about how each Chapter in the CourseBooks are organized by reading the introductory pages of the CourseBook itself.

Textbook

The material in the CourseBook is often made up of selected pieces of information on the course topic. These selected pieces reflect the parts your instructor feels are the most important and focus much effort on what you need to know to complete the assessments.

Some courses also have a textbook. This one does not. In courses that do have a textbook, you are required to obtain both the CourseBook and the Textbook as part of being successful in the class. The textbook will often provide an important depth to the information in the course that is not included in the CourseBook.

Other Links

In some instances you may find other specialized links on the main page of the course. These other links or folders will represent special components of the course that are better organized outside the Course Timeline.

Menu in Brightspace

When you are logged into a course in Brightspace, there is a menu that lists links across the top of the page.

This menu allows you to directly access specific functions within BS.

- **Home** - brings you back to the home page of the course where you will see any new course announcements.

- **Content** - brings you to the page where you will find the Overview/Syllabus and Course Timeline links.

- **Assignments** - brings you to choices so you can directly access any Discussions, Quizzes, or Assignments. This is a great place to go to check on your grades and feedback when you have been informed that something has been graded.

- **Communication** - brings you to options for communicating with your instructor. Be sure to check the section in the Overview/Syllabus page to see how you r instructor wishes to communicate with you.

- **Grades** - brings you to your grade book. Your grades will appear here as work is graded.

- **Resources** - brings you to options to sign up for tutoring, access BS help, and to access the KVCC Library.

Take sometime to familiarize yourself with how to navigate around the course. Just like moving to a new town, you want to spend some time just "driving around" to see where things are. You might even get lost, which is one of the best ways to get to know a place!

Learning Pathway

A "learning pathway" is the generic set of steps you will engage in to learn the material in this course. It is built into the structure of this course. Here is how to approach the organization and material in this course:

At the Start of Class

1. Read all the material posted in BS.

2. Read the syllabus.

3. Review the Course Timeline and make not of all due dates. Pay special attention to major projects that may need to managed over time.

Each Week

1. Lot into BS every day and check for announcements.

2. Plan ahead, but at the beginning of the week, be sure what is coming up and due in the next week.

3. Review the CourseBook for any Chapters that are due.

4. Review the corresponding textbook chapter for any that are due.

5. Participate in any online discussions (online classes) early in the week to create the best experience.

6. Complete the quizzes and assignments as indicated in the CourseBook.

7. Participate in online discussions (online courses) during the second half of the week to meet the expectations for response posts.

8. Plan ahead. Work ahead.

You can work ahead on most everything in this course, but do not post anything into future discussions. Post during the week when that discussion is due.

Assessment

This section describes the activities and assignments associated with this Chapter. Be sure to check with your instructor as to which ones you are expected to complete.

Note regarding Discussions: These activities are primarily geared toward students who are taking the course in either an Online or Hybrid format. It is expected that students will post an answer to the prompt contained in the section below and reply to at least two other students' posts in order to obtain full credit for the discussion. All posts must be substantive and contribute to the discussion.

Note regarding Assignments: These activities entail the creation of a "document" of sorts that needs to be sent to your instructor. Most of these may be papers. All papers must be submitted to the identified "Drop Box" for the assignment and must be in either Microsoft Word or PDF format. Pay attention to expectations such as title pages and APA formatting if these are indicated in the instructions.

Other assignments may entail different types of "documents" including presentations, artwork, charts, spreadsheets, and/or movies. Instructions on how to submit these will be included in the descriptions below

Though they will not be repeated, all of the above notes should be assumed in subsequent chapters, unless otherwise indicated.

Chapter 1 Discussion - Excitement

In this discussion I would like you to look through the course content and share which assignment you are most looking forward to completing in this class. Explain why.

Chapter 1 Quiz - Orientation

Answer the following questions:

1. My offline access to the CourseBook is:

   a) downloaded PDF.

   b) purchased Apple Books version.

   c) purchased print version.

   d) rented print version from college store.

2. Using the Course Timeline as a guide, describe your plan for completing all of the assigned work in this class.

Chapter 1 Assignment - Uploading

Purpose

The purpose of this assignment is to simply demonstrate your ability to construct a document and upload it successfully to the Chapter 1 Assignment drop box.

Skills and Knowledge

You will demonstrate the following skills and knowledge by completing this assignment:

1. Compose and format a document suitable for upload to the course drop box.

2. Successful submission of a file to the drop box.

Task

1. Compose a two page document in your word processor app of choice. The first page is the title page and the second page is a brief autobiographical sketch. Tell me whatever it is you would like me to know about you. Feel free to include a picture of yourself.

2. Save the file using the naming convention below.

3. Save the file as either a native MS Word file or as a PDF.

4. Upload the file to the drop box for Chapter 1 Assignment.

File Naming Convention

All digital drop boxes have certain rules about how to name files. You should not include spaces or special characters in the name of the file.

You also want to come up with a naming convention that works for your own effort at managing your files.

Here is an example that work for both your teachers and yourself.

(last name)(first initial)-(course)-(assignment).doc

If I were to submit this assignment, my file name would look like thisL

kavanaughm-PSY102-Ch01Assignment.doc

Criteria for Success

Use the rubric below as a guide to this assignment.

Title page   10 points
Includes the name of the assignment, class, your name, and date.

Autobiographical Sketch   70 points
A brief reflection on what you would like to tell about yourself.

Mechanics   20 points
Spelling, syntax, and organizational structure of the paper. Clear and organized.

KVCC and Psychology

2

Attention

Welcome to KVCC

Here is a very brief history, mission, vision, and values statement about KVCC!

Learning Outcomes

Upon completion of this Chapter, students should be able to:

1. Locate diverse resources available to students at KVCC.

2. Locate resources related to the Associates of Science in Psychology.

3. Develop a Student-Advisor Relationship Plan.

Teaching

Getting to Know KVCC

Kennebec Valley Community College is one of seven colleges under the Maine Community College System. Similar to the University of Maine System, the MCCS is a publicly funded college. This means that the State of Maine Legislature allocates funds to support the mission of the MCCS and allows us to offer opportunities for education and training at an affordable price.

Whether you are taking a class at a private school or a public one, the actual cost is the same. YOUR tuition has been partially funded by State of Maine tax dollars.

The KVCC Community

While KVCC is an institution, a school, it is far more a collection of people. It is the people of KVCC that make it such a unique and excellent organization to learn and work at. I started working at KVCC in 1997 and I have never seriously considered working anywhere else.

The KVCC community is made up of many different people in different roles. Just like any other large business, we have offices of administration, payroll, accounting, maintenance, and security. Because we are a school we have offices of advising, financial aid, student services, and of course, faculty. We also have services on campus for student enrichment and recreation that we hope will become a part of every student's experience at KVCC.

Students at KVCC

The last group of people I want to discuss are the students themselves. When I went to college for the first time, I was there with a bunch of young people. Mostly people aged 17 to 21. KVCC, and all the other community colleges, attract a much more diverse set of students.

At KVCC you will find "traditional" students (those coming right out of high school and up to 21 years old) but you will find other populations represented as well.

You may share a classroom with a home-schooled 16 year old, a recently retired senior, and a working mom or dad hoping to get a degree to change their career. You may also share a table with persons with disabilities, different gender identities, different racial and ethnic backgrounds, and certainly different views on the world!

This diversity is a STRENGTH at KVCC! Students don't only learn from their teachers and textbooks, they learn from each other. Having different points of view, even views in opposition to the teacher (horrors!) are not only present, but welcome!

Academic Culture

The reason that we have such harmony among such difference lays in our dedication to maintain an academic culture. An academic culture is one where knowledge is examined under the lens of logic, science, and critical reasoning. The pursuit of TRUTH, often a fruitless task is to examine ideas through this lens and focus are attentions on those that pass the tests. This is a discipline of thinking. It is a choice, that while you are at KVCC in class, you will take on the mantle of logic, science, and critical reasoning to examine the knowledge you encounter, the world around you, and even the assumptions that you came in with. The result of this volunteer activity is to become an **Educated Person**. The mission of the college is, essentially, to create educated people.

The Discipline of Psychology

Not only have chosen to study at KVCC, you have chosen the most wonderful, fascinating, and enlightening subject matter: Psychology!

The word "psychology" comes from two Greek terms: *psuchē* meaning "breath, life, soul, and now the mind" and *logos* meaning "speech, word, reason, and now knowledge". To study psychology is to study the knowledge of the mind!

The Greek letter Ψ (Psi) is the first letter in the word *psuchē* and it is the universal symbol for Psychology!

Earlier in this Chapter I talked about the "discipline" of the academic culture. This is a general expectations across all aspects of your college experience, but Psychology itself has it's own discipline as well.

The term "discipline", as you are likely thinking, has many meanings. It can refer to a punishment (such as a time out), a routine (such as my exercise regiment), or as a form of self-control. The "discipline of psychology" is both a routine (in terms of how we approach the interpretation of knowledge and how we seek new knowledge) and the mind-set and values that we align our thinking with.

The Routine

Simply put, the psychological discipline of "routine" involves a good dose of skepticism about claims without evidence and the need to support claims using methods of systematic and comprehensive observation (also known as the scientific method.

The Mind-Set

Our mindset is our set of beliefs that shape how you make sense of the world and of yourself. It shapes your personality, your activities, attitudes, and relationships.

The psychology mindset is most clearly outlined in the instructional goals of this program adapted from the guidelines for undergraduate Psychology programs published by the American Psychological Association. These guidelines guide the development of all the material in the different classes you will be taking in this program. At the beginning of this CourseBook you will find these outcomes listed along with the individual assignments in the course that align with the outcome.

Here they are:

Knowledge Base in Psychology

- Describe key concepts, principles, and over-arching themes in psychology.

- Develop a working knowledge of psychology's content domains.

- Describe applications of Psychology.

Scientific Inquiry and Critical Thinking

- Use scientific reasoning to interpret psychological phenomena.

- Demonstrate psychology information literacy.

- Engage in innovative and integrative thinking and problem solving.

- Interpret, design, and conduct basic psychological research.

- Incorporate sociocultural factors in scientific inquiry.

Ethical and Social Responsibility in a Diverse World

- Apply ethical standards to evaluate psychological science and practice.

- Build and enhance interpersonal relationships.

- Adopt values that build community at local, national, and global levels.

Communication

- Demonstrate effective writing for different purposes.

- Exhibit effective presentation skills for different purposes.

- Interact effectively with others.

Professional Development

- Apply psychological content and skills to career goals.

- Exhibit self-efficacy and self-regulation.

- Refine project management skills.

- Enhance teamwork capacity.

- Develop meaningful professional direction for life after graduation.

Through this program, you will be provided with opportunities to learn about and apply each aspect of this mindset. The vast majority of the assignments in all the Psychology courses you will take will be aligned in a way with these goals.

A Degree in Psychology

KVCC offers an Associates of Science in Psychology degree. It is the only associates degree of its kind in Maine.

You will be learning about the program and your path through it in this class! The key resources is the Psychology page on the KVCC website!

KVCC Associates in Science in Psychology

You have embarked on a path of learning and personal growth. This path has a lot of options and opportunities. But worry not! You have a guide by your side…a helping hand…you have an **Advisor**!

Getting (Good) Advice

I consider Psychology to be the "Master Science". I think this because all of the other sciences are the product of of our minds, and well, we study the mind itself!

Divisions of the APA

Psychology is also very diverse with lots of interests and intersections with other disciplines. Just take a look at the different Divisions with the American Psychological Association for a sense of what wide array of interests psychologists have (and these are just the big, official ones!)

To assist you in your journey through this program and beyond is your Academic Advisor…me!

Mark H. Kavanaugh, Ph.D.

I'm actually a Psychologist myself. I have lots of research interests and I have been studying psychology since 1985! I created this program at KVCC and I design the majority of the content you will be learning. Even though I might not teach all the classes, I'm responsible for all of them and you can reach out to me about your classes regardless of who you teacher is.

I'm your guide, advocate, advice giver, career counselor, and sometimes your reality checker. In this course we will begin to establish a relationship and define the way we will work together so you can accomplish your goals!

Assessment

Chapter 2 Discussion - KVCC PSY

Review all the pages in the KVCC Psychology website. Do you have any questions? Are you in the right place? What inspires you about studying Psychology? What do you want to do when you grow up?

Chapter 2 Quiz - KVCC

Since this class is online, we are going to NOT focus on getting to know the PHYSICAL campus of KVCC. We are going to explore the KVCC website! There is a LOT of information on the website and to help you learn how to navigate that site (and get to know KVCC as much as you can) I'm going to send you on a "Scavenger Hunt"

To complete this Scavenger Hunt activity, you will need to find the answers to some questions about KVCC. All of this information is located on the KVCC website...and you will have to click around and find it! When you have answered all the questions, go into the

Scavenger Hunt quiz below and submit your answers! Spelling counts and be sure to only give the specific information asked for. The quiz should grade itself!

I've included a "printable" version of these questions in the links below. Have fun!

Scavenger Hunt

Chapter 2 Assignment - Advising

Purpose

This assignment will help you establish your plan on how and when to communicate with your Academic Advisor.

Skills and Knowledge

You will demonstrate the following skills and knowledge by completing this assignment:

1. Contact your Academic Advisor through KVCC email.

2. Conduct a face-to-face or video conferencing meeting with your Academic Advisor.

3. Create an initial Academic Plan for completing the program.

Task

This assignment is simply the act of reaching out to your advisor, setting up a meeting, and establishing how you are going to work with your advisor to be successful in this program. Here are the steps:

1. Contact your advisor using your KVCC email account.

2. Set up and complete a 1:1 advising meeting either face-to-face or using video conferencing.

3. During that meeting you will complete an initial Academic Plan.

4. Write a brief paper about your strategy for keeping in touch with your Academic Advisor through your program.

Your paper will be written to meet the expectations outlined below.

Criteria for Success

Use the rubric below as a guide to this assignment.

Title page   10 points

Includes the name of the assignment, class, your name, and date.

Initial Academic Plan   20 points

Describe your initial Academic Plan.

Strategies   50 points

Summarize how you will keep in contact with your Academic Advisor. This may include specific times you will reach out and an action plan if you run into barriers.

Mechanics   20 points

Spelling, syntax, and organizational structure of the paper. Clear and organized.

24 Hours

3

Attention

24 Hours in a Day

There is an old adage, we all have the same 24 hours in a day. Our success is related to how we choose to use that time. It is campy. Sometimes we don't like to hear that. It is overused. Sometimes if feels like an insult. We all know people who have a lot more free time than we do to do things. But yet, the saying persists. It persists...because it is TRUE.

It's a simple fact. We are all on the planet Earth (i.e. a fixed 24+ hour day) and some people get a lot done while others don't get much done at all (and everything in-between.). Another fact is that when you get more done not only do people become more successful in the normal ways we think of success (work, money, power, career, etc.), they also get more done in the other ways; they love more, play more, enjoy more, relax more, walk the dog more, etc.

In this Chapter I'm going to introduce the concept that we are often taught to manage our time in the wrong way.

Nearly every time management seminar or training I've been to discussed the need to schedule time to get things done. For instance, if I course reading, 3 quizzes, 4 online discussion, two papers and an exam on Friday, I might look at the time I have off from work and block out some times in my calendar.

- Monday - 9 AM - 9:30 AM - Reading
- Monday - 7 PM - 8 PM - Discussions 1 and 2
- Monday - 8 PM - 10 PM - Paper #1
- Tuesday - 9 AM - 9:30 AM - Reading
- Tuesday - 7 PM - 8 PM - Discussions 3 and 4
- Wednesday - 8 PM - 10 PM - Paper #2
- Thursday - 8 PM - 10 PM - Prep for Exam
- Friday - 8 PM - 10 PM - Complete Quizzes

If you are like me…on each of these days you have another thing scheduled after 9:30 on Monday morning (like going to work) and after 8 PM on Tuesday (get the kids ready for school).

Some of you might be looking at this and saying, wow, I really wish I could do just that!! Either way, there is a lot wrong with scheduling time to get your coursework done this way.

The most important thing that is wrong with this is, what if you don't get the paper done on Monday from 8 PM - 10 PM? You have scheduled that time with expectations to get it done and have no other time put aside for that activity. You underestimated how long it would take, you ran into trouble getting information for your paper, etc. etc. etc.

Let's take a look at how I try to manage my own time and see if that might be a better path for you. I am never perfect at this, I fail daily, but it still works.

Learning Outcomes

Upon completion of this Chapter, students should be able to:

1. Discuss the fallacy of "blocks of time" within time management practice.

2. Apply metacognition to the development of a plan for completion of academic tasks.

3. Produce a plan for balance between school, work, family, and play.

Teaching

Managing Time

I'm going to take this Chapter to talk about some of the important aspects of time management that I have learned. While I'm asking you to demonstrate your understanding of this process you are not obligated to use this method if it is not your style. It may be that through this process you will find a system that works for you. Perhaps you even have one already!

Scheduled Time and Productivity Time

The first distinction in how we use time has to do with our time commitments to certain activities. These activities include work, family time, relaxation, meetings, and sleep. These are the "fixed" aspects of our schedule.

For instance, if you work a regular 9am - 5pm job, then you would block this out as committed time. You could also block out family time, relaxation time, a night out with friends, and bed time.

Weekly Activity Schedule

Truthfully, you want to start your day as early as possible…like at 4-5 am.

Week Beginning: _____

	Monday	Tuesday	Wednesday	Thursday	Friday	Saturday	Sunday
8 to 9 am							
9 to 10							
10 to 11							
11 to 12 pm							
12 to 1			WORK				
1 to 2							
2 to 3							
3 to 4							
4 to 5							Relax
5 to 6							Family
6 to 7							
7 to 8					Friends		
8 to 10							
10 to 12 am			Bed Time				

Centre for

Clinical Interventions
·Psychotherapy·Research·Training·

Everything else, the times indicated by the arrows, is when you have the opportunity to be productive and address your to-do lists!

Note - It is not uncommon for busy people to wake up very early in the morning in order to maximize their productivity time. It may even open up opportunities for more fun and relaxing times later in the day.

As you consider this aspect of your time management, you may have to think about some of the commitments that you have. Do achieve your goals, can you actually keep all these commitments? Are you going to have to let some go (at least for a while) so you can do well in school, or to get other more important things done? Can you delegate other people in the home to do things (yes, you can and that is what it means to have a family that supports your goals)?

To free up more productivity time you might have to give up on having the most tidy house on the planet, watching TV, going out often, having friends over, partying, drinking, drugs, etc. Yup, it is productivity time, time to put childish things away.

To-Do Lists

I am a huge fan of to-do lists. Like really. A single to-do list can be very overwhelming. If you were going to plan a while week and all the things you need to get done, it might make you want to simply go back to bed and wake up in 7 days! I use topical to-do lists in order to get things done in regard to different aspects of my life.

Personally, I use an app that is both on my computer and my phone. I use this app to manage a whole bunch of individual lists including my work, music, writing, and other projects.

I also have a master list of my daily to-do items. I will explain how I create this master list shortly.

Large Projects

One of the reasons I have a lot of different lists is because I break down large projects into small steps. My brain rarely allows me to work consistently on one thing for a very long time so I break it up into ordered pieces and then I insert them individually into my master to-do list.

This can sometimes take some thinking and some trial and error to be able to understand a large task well enough to break it down into its parts. With practice, though, you will find that you get better and better at it.

This applies to any sort of large task whether it is a paper to do for school or the planting of a garden. Your ability to divide up the task into manageable parts and the put an action plan in place is your key to success.

Metacognition

This process of thinking about how we might go about a task, understanding our own learning methods, our own strengths and limitations...all of this is referred to as **metacognition**.

Managing activities of varying complexity (some are just a single to-do list item - "call mom" - others are much more complex - "write the grant proposal").

High and Low Cognitive Load

If you look at your list of things to do you may see that you can divide them all into one of two categories. You have tasks that are simple and can be done easily (such as mowing the lawn or posting a reply in a discussion board.). You have others that are going to engage you a lot more and require more thinking (preparing an outline for a paper or practicing a speech). These differences represent variance in **cognitive load**.

Picture your brain lifting weights. High cognitive load activities require your brain to work very hard.

Activities that tax our brains feel like "work"...we might not even like doing parts of them, yet they are things we need to do to be successful

Low cognitive load activities are easy to do, they happen automatically, and you are likely good at them and may even enjoy them.

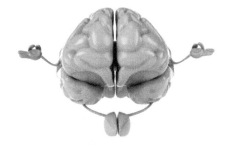

Cognitive Load and Procrastination

Cognitive load is ONE of the factors that contributes to procrastination. We all like to feel productive and we can do this by getting all those low cognitive load items off our list. We can praise ourselves for keeping busy and getting things done, but some things, often important and graded things, get continually put aside. It makes sense! Who wants to practice a speech when you can do the dishes and actually SEE the results of your efforts! And, well, you need a clean house, others depend on you doing the dishes, image what people would think knowing you have dirty dishes in your sink...dang it, doing the dishes is AMERICAN!

Do you see where I went with that? We can actually convince ourselves that our long list of low cognitive tasks are more important that our high cognitive tasks and we will end up failing. We even go far as telling ourselves that if it wasn't for those dishes getting dirty all the time, I would have done well on the speech!

Here is my major point...you need to get them both done, but in my plan, the low cognitive tasks are rewards you give yourself for completing high cognitive tasks! Yes, you are going to complete that paper outline and you are going to reward yourself with...doing laundry? Stay tuned...

Organize

Take all the items on your list and break them out into two different lists. One contains high cognitive tasks the other low cognitive tasks. You can just label them on the same paper if you like.

Note - Remember, if you have a big task that has been divided into smaller steps, some of those steps might require different cognitive effort. Label them in this way.

Prioritize

Look at each item in each list (high and low) and put them in order of importance. This is hard to do...but don't worry, you can change the priority, but you need to first list them from most important to least important.

I'm going to make up a list of high and low cognitive tasks in order of importance.

High Cognitive Load	Low Cognitive Load
Work on writing Chapter 3 in CourseBook	Dishes
Prepare presentation to KVCC Foundation	Cat Litter
Review Student Progress in Classes	Mulch Front Lawn
Prepare Psychobabble Video	Set up Stereo
Clear KVCC Email	Set up Racquetball Games
Matrix for Experiential Education	Clean out Garage
Standard Template for CourseBooks	Bike Ride
Grading	Practice Guitar
Review MHRT/C non-Credit Training	Weed Section of Garden

This comes from my actual to-do lists for today, as I am writing this! As you can see the items on the left require deeper thinking and are more challenging that the ones on the right. I usually enjoy all of these tasks, but when I'm hungry or tired, even things I like to do are not so appealing!

The Magic

So, here is how it works!

Each day…

1. I organize the most important high and low activities for the day.

2. I rank order them in terms of high to low priority. (This changes day to day because I have daily things, like checking in on my classes that are always #1 for the day.)

3. I make a single master list that alternates between high and low activities. Behaviorally, I "reward" myself for completing a high cognitive load task by assigning myself a low cognitive load task.

4. Each time I have unscheduled productivity time, I return to this list and pick up where I left off.

5. At the end of the day, I always have things left over and these may become high priority for the next day.

6. I celebrate each day that I feel I get a good deal of things done, and I don't get down on myself for having a rough day once in a while. I have amazing days, and days where I can't seem to get much done….but…

7. I do this EVERY DAY. And I get a LOT DONE.

I'm really harnessing a lot of psychology here. Some tasks take more effort, less effort tasks, by comparison are rewarding. I have the other reward of checking off the box, and I have a plan for how to deal with unscheduled, potentially productive time.

My to-do list now looks like this:

To Do List
Work on writing Chapter 3 in CourseBook
Dishes
Prepare Presentation to KVCC Foundation
Cat Litter
Review Student Progress in Classes
Mulch Front Lawn
Prepare Psychobabble Video
Set Up Stereo
Clear KVCC Email
Set up Racquetball Games
Matrix for Experiential Education
Clean out Garage
Standard Template for CourseBooks
Bike Ride
Grading
Practice Guitar
Review MHRT/C non-credit Training
Weed Section of Garden

I progress though this list during all the unscheduled productivity times and get as much done as possible.

Let me point out that there are items here that are part of separate lists that include steps in a larger project. I have made those items bold. Tomorrow, I will fill in those spots with the next step in those particular projects so that I do one each day.

Sometimes I move things around a bit if progress is slow to be sure the things that I really need to get done today, get done today. The "review of student progress" and "bike ride" are about to get moved higher in priority.

Now that I have completed my work on writing Chapter 3 in this CourseBook, I'm going to do the dishes!

Assessment

Chapter 3 Discussion - Time

Share your own successes and failures regarding time management. Share if you have a system that consistently works, even if it is different than the one I consider in this Chapter.

Chapter 3 Assignment - Plan

Purpose

This assignment will allow you to demonstrate the ability to plan a week in accordance with the model that is described in this Chapter. It is not necessary for you to actually use this model to manage your time, but you can pick and choose parts that are working and customize your own approach.

Skills and Knowledge

You will demonstrate the following skills and knowledge by completing this assignment:

1. Develop both high and low cognitive load to-do lists.

2. Schedule blocks of both scheduled (work, play, family, etc.) and productivity time.

3. Produce a master to do list that will guide you through the productivity times in your schedule.

Task

1. As described in the Chapter, you will need to create two prioritized to-do lists. One will consist of the high cognitive load things you need to get done and the other will consist of a prioritized list of the the low cognitive load things you need to get done.

2. Create a graphic that encompasses a week of your schedule. You may use a template weekly calendar if you wish.

3. Block off all the fixed scheduled time that you have already committed. Be as detailed as possible so you can know when your productivity time begins and ends.

4. Merge your high and low cognitive to-do lists into a master to-do list ordered by altering between high and low cognitive activities.

This becomes the list that you turn to when time opens up for you to become productive. Right up until your next fixed scheduled time.

Criteria for Success

Use the rubric below as a guide to this assignment.

Title page   10 points

Includes the name of the assignment, class, your name, and date.

Two Lists   30 points

Two separate lists. One list has high cognitive load tasks in it and the other list has low cognitive load tasks in it. Items are in order of priority and cover the week. Be sure to include daily items as well.

Calendar   10 points

Calendar is a table with fixed committed times identified.

Master To-Do List   30 points

This list will alternate between high and low cognitive load items.

Mechanics   20 points

Spelling, syntax, and organizational structure of the paper. Clear and organized.

Technology

4

Attention

My To-Do List App

In the last Chapter I teased the fact that I actually use an app to manage my to-do lists and engage in my time and task management system. While I have been a very long time fan of hand-written lists (I used to buy Franklin Planners every year!), I found that my list had to be reorganized all the time. It is a **dynamic** to-do list where I change the order of things through the day in response to my productivity and the passage of time.

After exploring a LOT of different apps, I found one that lives both on my computer and on my phone (it could be on my watch too, but that is simply too much!)

That app is called **Things**. This is for Mac and iOS only.

Things is a map that allows me to not only create to-do lists but to also:

- Create Projects.
- Organize multiple lists into each Project.
- Add bullet steps to a single item.
- Incorporate due dates for anything.

I don't even use all the tools that are in the app. In addition, the database that supports the app is stored in my Drop Box account. The apps on my computer and my phone (and potentially my watch) access this database so any updates to the lists are communicated to all of my devices!

Joyfully, my entire technology world revolves around Apple products. I have multiple laptops, desktops, iPads, an iPhone, and an Apple Watch. The care that goes into these products and how they work together convinces me every day that these products are amazing. BTW, I also have an Apple TV.

You may find your own digital tools or you may have yellow sticky notes pasted all over your wall (yup, did that too for a while)...but finding the best tool for you is critical. Here are some links and a screen shot of my Things screen for today.

Things by CultureCode

Franklin-Covey Planners

This is a screen shot from my Things app as it appears today. This helps me organize a LOT of simultaneous projects. No...I don't own stock in this app!

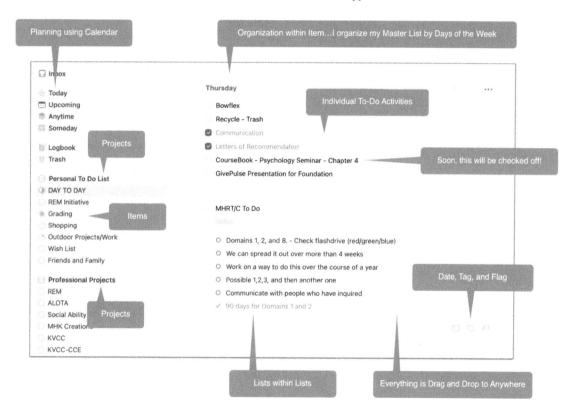

Planning using Calendar

Organization within Item...I organize my Master List by Days of the Week

Projects

Items

Projects

Individual To-Do Activities

Soon, this will be checked off!

Date, Tag, and Flag

Lists within Lists

Everything is Drag and Drop to Anywhere

Inbox
Today
Upcoming
Anytime
Someday

Logbook
Trash

Personal To Do List
DAY TO DAY
REM Initiative
Grading
Shopping
Outdoor Projects/Work
Wish List
Friends and Family

Professional Projects
REM
ALOTA
Social Ability
MHK Creation
KVCC
KVCC-CCE

Thursday

Bowflex
Recycle - Trash
Communication
Letters of Recommendation
CourseBook - Psychology Seminar - Chapter 4
GivePulse Presentation for Foundation

MHRT/C To Do
Notes

○ Domains 1, 2, and 8. - Check flashdrive (red/green/blue)
○ We can spread it out over more than 4 weeks
○ Work on a way to do this over the course of a year
○ Possible 1,2,3, and then another one
○ Communicate with people who have inquired
✓ 90 days for Domains 1 and 2

Learning Outcomes

Upon completion of this Chapter, students should be able to:

1. Utilize MS Office tools including Word, Excel, and Powerpoint.

2. Identify methods of using other productivity tools.

3. Utilize ZOOM tools to conduct an online meeting.

4. Explore the use of Apple iPad devices and apps for learning.

Teaching

Technology

First, we need to have a conversation about what "technology" means. Despite the fact that I will talking mostly about computers and apps, technology is really any tool that helps you get a job done. We are tool makers as a species and we create tools to make our life easier and/or to do things beyond the physical abilities we have. (Cheetahs have no need to evolve into car-creating animals because they can run fast enough to get the job done.)

Seeing Technology as a Tool

A person walks into a hardware store. They approach the counter and ask to be shown options for a drill. One might jump to the conclusion that the customer is looking for a drill. But, technically, they are not. A wise and savvy employee may ask..."What are you looking for a drill to do?"

Now, as a tool, a drill can do many things:

- Make a hole

- Drive a screw

- Drive a nut around a screw

- Take out a stuck screw

- Art (attache a brush with paint and turn that baby on and watch!)

- Cleaner (attache a brush)

- Mix drinks

- Play guitar (yes, Eddie did that as well...)

Another guitar player, Paul Gilbert, takes this further!

Set up your Drill like Paul Gilbert

Back to the hardware store...

Depending on what the customer wants to do, the employee can guide his to the **right** drill or even another tool that will do the job better. Having a clear idea what we are trying to do will often help us pick the best tool for the job.

I have curated some of these for students who are in the Psychology degree program. These may change as better tools become available or changes in the program necessitate new tools, but we will see.

Now I'm going to outline the best technology you will need to be successful in this program! I'm also going to get very opinionated...you can take that advice or not, but I do have thoughts about what are the best tools to use when it comes to technology!

Tools for the Associates of Science in Psychology

Tasks - Accessing the Internet, Running Applications, and Creating Assignments.

Tool - Laptop Computer and/or Tablet

One of the first tools you will need is, of course, a computer. All of the courses in this program require that you access the Internet and that you produce digital versions of assignments using specific applications (such as MS Word).

MK Wisdom

My favorite tools are, of course, Apple products. I find they work more reliably, no viruses, and they last longer. I have used Windows and Android devices and the are inferior. While Apple products can be more expensive, they are usually better quality builds, they come with other tools you will need for free, and they work together very well.

I have a laptop, iPad, and an iPhone and I am very pleased with these. You should get the best version of these tools you can afford. This is an investment because you do not want your tool itself to be a barrier in your learning.

Task - Writing Papers, Doing Statistics, and Designing Presentations

Tool - An office suite of applications that includes a word processor, spreadsheet, and presentation software.

The most popular set of tools out there that meets this criteria is Microsoft Office. With MS Office you get Word (word processor), Excel (spreadsheets), and PowerPoint (presentations).

 Office 365

All students at KVCC are provided with free access to Microsoft Office! We have a deal with them that allow currently registered students to download all the Office apps to their computer and to any mobile device (there are versions of Word, Excel, and PowerPoint that will work on our tablet and/or phone.)

This tool will also give you access to other Microsoft apps such as Teams (KVCC uses this to hold virtual meetings), OneDrive (online file storage), OneNote (organize information), and Outlook (email client).

To access these tools you need to visit the link below and use your KVCC user name and password to register.

www.office.com

MK Wisdom

Despite the fact that I am an Apple super-fan, I really prefer MS Office to the tools that Apple provides, with one exception...later.

MS Word is a great word processing tool, it is universal, it has templates to help you write in APA format, and the files can be uploaded to our learning management system and read directly in the interface (instead of having to download the file.)

MS Excel is a fantastic tool for organizing all sorts of information and creating calculated tables, graphs, and charts. The Statistics for Psychology course uses Excel and a special plug-in to teach about the different statistical tests used in Psychology. It is important that you have a version of Excel that supports this plug-in.

MS PowerPoint is OK. PowerPoint is presentation software that allows you to organize information into slides that you display while giving a presentation. You can use animations and transitions between slides to add a dynamic effect to your speech!

However, Apple does have an office suite as well. It is made up of three applications, Pages (word processor), Numbers (spreadsheets), and Keynote (presentations). Keynote is a far superior presentation software when compared to PowerPoint. Not because of any specific function, both are very capable programs...but because it LOOKS BETTER.

Personally, I use MS Word, MS Excel, and Keynote on all my devices. Keynote is only available for Mac and iOS, but just like you can access free online versions of MS Office apps, you can also sign up to access free versions of Apple's apps using the link below and your Apple ID.

Access Apple iCloud

Another popular set of tools for these purposes is Google Docs. **Please do not use Google Docs in any of my courses!**

This has been continually problematic to me and while they apps are functional, they are feature anemic for professional use.

If you do wish to use another tool, even Google Docs, it is important that you convert your original files into one that can be opened and usable in our learning management system. Convert your files to MS Office format or to PDF. These conversion options are usually available in all applications. Even if you are using Pages from Apple, convert your files to PDF and submit those versions.

Task - Video Conferencing, Virtual Attendance at Meetings, Group Meetings, Communication with your Advisor.

Tool - Video Conferencing Software

COVID-19 ushered in a time where we all had to get used to working at a distance. As frustrating and different as this was for many of us, we also developed skills related to video conferencing and how to be productive in this environment.

By far, the most popular tool on the market is ZOOM. ZOOM is an app that lives on your computer or mobile device that utilizes your camera, microphone, and a connection to other ZOOM users to allow for real time video conferencing. Just like having a face-to-face discussion…almost!

Access and sign up for ZOOM

MK Wisdom

We have all had to learn how to be better users of technology over these years, and ZOOM is not exception. Here are some things to keep in mind when you are going to use ZOOM as a professional tool.

- Dress professionally, even if it is only from the waste up.

- Be mindful of what is in back of you, we can all see that.

- Make sure others who may wander into the room know that you are in a virtual room with other people looking.

- Audio is actually more important that video. Makes sure your audio settings are good and possibly get a good microphone.

- **Do not** walk around, eat, answer a phone, pat your cat/dog/goat, engage in unrelated work, deal with your kids, apply cosmetics, do your hair, look for food in your teeth, fall asleep, look really bored, swear, undress, get into an argument with someone, invite non-members into the meeting, cough/sneeze/clean your nose, brush your teeth, exercise, engage in excessive movement, walk out of the room, or smoke/do drugs/drink alcohol while your camera or your mic are still on (I have experienced ALL of these during ZOOM meetings.)

- Learn how to use ZOOM. Just like any other tool you need to master how to configure the settings. Your impression is going out, make it a professional one. ZOOM itself has great video tutorials on how to use their software. Watch ALL OF THEM.

Setting Up the Shot

In order to have the best ZOOM experience possible you need to do the following:

- Conduct the ZOOM meeting in a quiet room with little to no distractions.

- If you are using a laptop, phone or tablet, place the tablet on a table and prop it up. Do not hold it in your hand or sit it on your lap as it will constantly move.

- Make sure there are no competing sounds that might be loud on the receiver end even though you have got used to it (think loud appliances and generators.)

- Center yourself in the middle of the outgoing frame of your camera.

Lighting

You should be FACING the light source (window, light fixture, etc.) with little to no sources of light behind you. Your camera will adjust its settings to the light behind you and you will be very very unnaturally dark and invisible.

Here are a couple of graphics to explain these expectations.

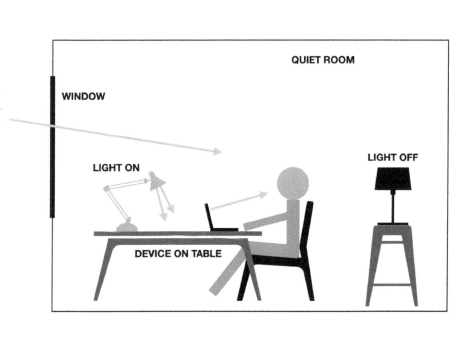

YOU ON CAMERA

  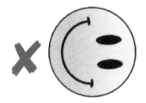

MK thinks you need an iPad

Having an iPad is optional. But, there are lots of good reasons to have one (along with a good laptop, preferably a MacBook Air or MacBook Pro)

As you may already know, the CourseBooks for all my classes are available in multiple formats. You can download a PDF copy directly from within Brightspace. You can get a printed copy from Amazon or our campus store. Or…you can purchase an interactive, EPUB formatted version directly from Apple Books.

None of the versions of the CourseBooks restrict access to anything. All the links work either by clicking on them or scanning the QR codes with your device. The advantage of the EPUB version is really with the embedded movies. When you select a movie to play in the EPUB version, it plays right in the CourseBook, it does not take you to a website (at least not all the time).

All the coding that goes into creating this digital book has been optimized for the iPad. The book is more responsive, scrolls better, resizes text better, and provides digital note-taking, highlighting, and even reading of the text.

Not only is the iPad the ideal tool to read these Course-Books, the iPad is also a powerful and very portable learning and performance platform. Free and very low cost apps enable you to:

- Take and edit pictures.
- Scan documents.
- Draw and paint with lifelike pencils, paints, and brushes.
- Record and edit movies.
- Listen to and Compose original music.
- Record and transcribe lectures.
- Create interactive instructional animations.
- Code and program.
- Watch movies.
- Scan and edit 3D models.
- Navigate nearly anywhere in the world.
- Create and subscribe to PodCasts.
- Plan your garden and landscaping.
- Improve your mental health.
- Exercise with professional trainers.
- Plan a road trip.
- Explore the cosmos.
- Keep up on Instagram and TikTok.
- Engage in brain training.
- Meditate.
- Email, chat, surf the web.
- …and, of course, have a very cool to-do list routine!

Simply get the best one you an afford!

Assessment

Chapter 4 Discussion - My Tech

In this discussion I want you to share the technology that you feel comfortable with and how you plan to adapt it to this program. What is your favorite tool?

If you are using tools other than the ones I have described, how do you plan on using them to learn in the class?

Chapter 4 Assignment - ZOOM

Purpose

The purpose of this assignment is to utilize ZOOM to schedule and run a ZOOM conference.

Skills and Knowledge

You will demonstrate the following skills and knowledge by completing this assignment:

1. Installation of ZOOM on your devices.

2. Creation of a scheduled ZOOM meeting.

3. Send out a link to individuals you wish to meet with on ZOOM.

4. Conduct the ZOOM session and teach/demonstrate the following ZOOM skills:

   - Share your screen.
   - Others share screen.
   - Share a single app window.
   - Change you displayed name.
   - Use the chat function.
   - Use the whiteboard function.
   - Turn camera/mic on and off.
   - Blur and/or change background.

Task

For this assignment you are going to download and create an account with ZOOM on your devices.

Familiarize yourself with the functions and tools within ZOOM.

Communicate with your advisor to set up an agreed time to meet.

Create the ZOOM meeting in advance and send the link to the ZOOM meeting to your advisor.

When you meet with your advisor you will teach and demonstrate how to do the list of skills outlined in the Skills and Knowledge section.

Criteria for Success

This will be graded on a pass/fail (0 or 100) basis.

The Three Rs

5

Attention

Readin', Writin', and 'Rithmetic

Technology is cool, but those are just tools to help you master the content. In the early years of education, what you needed to know was how to read, write, and do math...these basic skills were thought to be the most useful in life.

They still are!

Likely you already know how to read and write, and I know some of you love math, but we are going to focus on the Three Rs in Psychology:

Reading peer reviewed literature and technical writing.
Writing in APA style.
Mathematics as it applies to statistics.

Learning Outcomes

Upon completion of this Chapter, students should be able to:

1. Utilize library resources to locate peer-reviewed psychological literature.

2. Provide an oral presentation summarizing a specific peer-reviewed psychological article.

3. Identify resources for applying APA writing style.

4. Discuss the uses of statistics in the field of psychology.

Teaching

Psychological Epistemology

What a phrase that is!! Let's dissect it. We know that Psychology is the "knowledge of the mind"...Epistemology is "the methods, validity, and scope of what is known" in a particular field. In a way, we can approach this like a Jeopardy statement.

"Psychology for $200, please"

Answer - Psychological Epistemology

Question - How do we know what we know in the field of Psychology?

Methods

Methods describe the way the field of Psychology discovers stuff. The methods used are scientifically based and subject to review to ensure they were done correctly. A psychologist cannot simply walk into the mall and start making assumptions about how people are acting. They need to implement the Scientific Method.

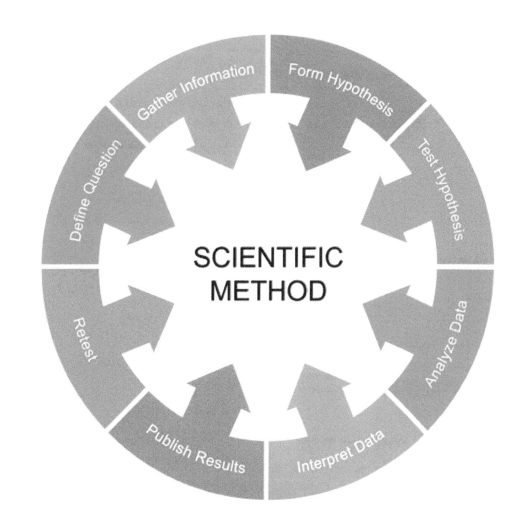

From this graphic you can see the methods of science start with…

1. **Define Question** - Create clear definition of variables and measures.

2. **Gather Information** - What do we already know?

3. **Form Hypothesis** - What do we think we will find based on what we already know?

4. **Test Hypothesis** - Gather data.

5. **Analyze Data** - Apply statistics and/or other analyses.

6. **Interpret Data** - Draw conclusions as to if your analysis supports your hypothesis or not.

7. **Publish Results** - Have others review your work for quality and validity.

8. **Retest** - Redo the study, ask new/related questions…over and over and over.

Validity

Validity is a measure as to how much of what we discover is true, real, and helpful. There are a number of ways in which we discuss validity.

- **Face Validity** - it "looks" right.

- **Construct Validity** - the way we define our variables seems to actually identify what we are tying to study.

- **Internal Validity** - our ideas work cohesively together.

- **External Validity** - another measure of our construct correlates with our measure.

- **Is it important?** - We want to ask this question early!

- **Is it useful?** - We want to ask this question early!

So far we have described methods as being the way we go about gathering about people and the way they think and making sure that what we write about, say, and conclude is valid. But there is one other very important aspect of Psychological Epistemology…scope.

No…not that kind of scope!
Though it IS related to it.

Scope is the definition of what we DO study and what we DO not study. Psychology studies a lot of things, but there are lots of things that it does not study. In addition, sometimes we purposefully LIMIT the scope of what we are studying in order to focus our work.

Here are some examples.

1. In general, the scope of the field of psychology is **limited** to behavior we can directly observe, or infer indirectly by testing.

2. A lifespan psychologist would **limit** scope from conception to death and not necessarily study any notions of what might happen before and after these points.

3. Biopsychology **limits** it's interpretations to those that can be explained by biology, chemistry, and evolution.

4. Psychologists should **limit** the scope of their practice to those things they have specific and substantive training in.

As you can see, scope is often spoken of in terms of professional **limits** that we place on the what we are looking at, our explanations, and applications.

Sometimes we can choose to **expand** the scope of a study.

1. A study has revealed that a new medication for treating OCD in adolescence has been effective. We might want to **expand** the scope of the study to include older populations.

2. Walking in the woods has been found to be helpful to many individuals who are experiencing stress. We might want to **expand** the scope of our study to other potentially relaxing activities such as walking on a beach.

3. Social Psychologists **expand** the scope of their practice by taking into consideration the knowledge we have of Sociology and behavior in groups.

4. A scope of a test designed to measure reading speed can **expand** to also measure reading comprehension.

All this said, there is a nice safe way to ensure that you are reading material that has been put together based on accepted methods, validity, and scope.

The Psychological Literature

The Psychological Literature (or simply "Literature") is the body of written work that has been established over years and years of scientific study. All together it comprises the body of knowledge in a specific field.

The literature is found in many places, but mostly in the form of academic journals. These journals can be both general and very specific in scope. They are published by professional organizations and publishers such as the American Psychological Association (APA), Association for Psychological Science (APS), and Sage Publishing.

As with all writing, these publishers have an audience in mind, and it is not you...it is barely me! Journals are how scientists **publish results**, as we talked about in the methods, and the target audience is "other scientists".

None-the-less...we are going to look at them anyway!

Professional Organizations

APA and APS are both professional organizations to which psychologists can belong. The APA is the largest professional organization in the world, despite it's "American" name! By becoming members of these organizations, psychologists can subscribe to any number of journals.

The American Psychological Association not only has general journals that cover featured work going all over the field of psychology, every Division within the APA also has one or two journals. This allows members to keep up on the most current work available in the field. Additional, and more timely, resources are also available online.

Luckily, as a student, you have access to these journals through databases that the college purchases. The library also participates with other libraries in the state to subscribe additional resources.

Even though research is not the focus of many community colleges, the KVCC Library is a very good research library because of all the data bases and partnerships that they have.

Access our Library and our Librarians

Professional Writing

As you begin to encounter these journal articles, you are going to see that, in many ways, they are similar to one another. In order to simplify the expectations of writing professional articles, many publishers have adopted the writing guidelines established by the American Psychological Association. In fact, APA style is the most common expectation for writing style in college.

In this class, you were asked to purchase a copy of the manual published by the APA to communicate APA writing style to professionals and students in college.

Concise Guide to APA Style (7th Ed.)
The Official APA Style Guide for Students

Reading through this guide is really not a bad idea. There is a lot in her that has to do with choice of words, how to create your "academic voice", along with formatting your title pages, in-text citations, tables, images, graphs, and references correctly.

Statistics

Simply defined, statistics is a tool that is used in research to quantify, explain, analyze, and make decisions based on numerical data (for the most part). Much of what we know about psychology is due to research that has attempted to measure different human traits. We have tests for intelligence, personality, ambition, stress, depression, imagination, and all sorts of other skills and qualities. Many of these tests produce a number that we can use to compare different individuals' abilities.

This **descriptive** aspect of numbers allows us to understand the quantity of something. How much intelligence or stress someone has. Another type of statistics is referred to as **projective**. Projective tests allow us to predict one trait by knowing another one (correlations and regressions) and to determine if there is a cause-effect relationship between two factors (experiments). Numbers allow us to determine if something is really there are if it is just a coincidence.

Statistics is also a whole field in itself. It is used in other sciences (chemistry, genetics, physics, etc.) and is one of the principle mathematics that define the "language of science." Take a look at this article.

Almasri, F., Hewapathirana, G.I., Alhashem, F., Daniel, C.E., and Lee, N. (2022) The effect of gender composition and pedagogical approach on major and non-major undergraduates biology students' achievement. *Interactive Learning Environments.* AHEAD-OF-PRINT, 1-33

This article uses statistics to provide evidence that factors such as gender composition (mixed gender vs. single gender class composition), learning method (traditional vs. collaborative), and student type (major vs. non-major) contributed to students' overall achievement.

- Hypotheses - pp. 9-10
- Descriptive Statistics - p. 11
- Projective Statistics (including Independent Samples t tests, ANOVA, and Paired Samples t tests) tables - pp. 13-15

This is just an example of how statistics are used in research to address hypotheses in a study. You will be learning about all the statistical tests when you take Statistics for Psychology!

Assessment

Chapter 5 Discussion - Statistics

There are three major types of studies that you will encounter in the literature of this field. Qualitative Studies, Quantitative Studies, and Meta-analysis. The vast majority of them will be Quantitative Studies.

Look up these terms and discuss how all three could contribute to an understanding of a topic. Also discuss why Quantitative Studies (those that utilize numerical measurements of variables and statistics, seem to be more influential.)

Chapter 5 Quiz - APA Reference

1. Write out the APA style reference to your article.

(You have unlimited chances on this quiz as I will continue to grade it as a ZERO until it is perfect!)

Chapter 5 Assignment - An Article

Purpose

The purpose of this assignment is to demonstrate the ability to locate a full-text, peer reviewed article utilizing the campus library services. Specifically, you will be utilizing the search tools in the EBSCO database to locate your article.

In addition, you will create a slide presentation, and record a brief presentation on the article.

Being able to locate, read, and demonstrate understanding of the psychological literature is key to your success in this program and in the field of Psychology. This type of writing is not easy to read. You, actually, are not the intended audience, other psychologists are. But as you train to become psychologists you can experience the unique format and style of professional writing in the field.

Skills and Knowledge

You will demonstrate the following skills and knowledge by completing this assignment:

2. Establishing contact with librarians to assist you with your search.

3. Identify a search strategy within EBSCO to find an article related to your selected topic.

4. Identify the individual parts of the article and their general contents.

5. Create a slide presentation describing the various parts of the article.

6. Record a voice presentation into the slide show discussing each part of the peer-reviewed article.

7. Demonstrate the ability to create an APA formatted reference to the article and include it in the presentation.

Task

As you can see in the Skills and Knowledge section, there are many parts to this assignment, culminating with you submitting a slide show with an oral presentation embedded into it. While the assignment has many parts, each part is relatively easy to accomplish. You may have to reach out to our Librarians for help, learn about how to record into your device, and learn how to successfully present complex information.

Step 1

You will need to select a topic of interest that you have related to the field of Psychology. You may already have one or you may have too many...or you may not have a clue where to begin! Let me give you a starting point.

Here is a link to a list of "controversial" questions that use as a starting point for both my Introduction to Psychology and my Introduction to Sociology courses. Nearly all of these topics have both psychological and sociological significance.

Controversial Topics

Step 2

Now you need to find an article (any article) that is related to your selected topic. For this assignment, the article does not need to specifically answer your question, it can be simply about the topic. For example, if you selected the topic:

"Should corporations be granted personhood?"

You might simply look up an article related to personhood. You could also look up an article about related topics like Artificial Intelligence and personhood.

The Chapter contains some lessons about using the EBSCO database to find peer reviewed articles, but feel free to reach out to our librarians directly to help. they can make sure that you learn how to use the right search terms, and how to limit your search to full-text and to the age of the article.

Step 3

For this part of the assignment you are going to read your entire article (don't worry, it is supposed to be confusing!). While you are reading you are going to note the typical structure of an article like this. Usually, if it is a Quantitative Study, you will find parts of the article like this:

- Abstract
- Introduction
- Hypotheses
- Methods
- Results
- Discussion
- References

Keep in mind that there are all kinds of articles out there and they may not contain all of these parts and they may have other parts. The point is to see that the article is divided into parts.

Step 4

Now you are ready to create your slide presentation! You will create a slide show using PowerPoint or Keynote and edit the presentation to briefly describe each part of the article.

Each slide should be very simple in layout. No one wants to reach a slide with all sorts of text on it.

Use the "Notes" feature in the software to write out the details of each part of the article for each slide. The presentation should be neat, professional, and aesthetically attractive.

Step 5

Both PowerPoint and Keynote have the ability to have you narrate your presentation and record it right into the file itself. This is the file you will be submitting to me to get graded. Your slides, notes in the notes section, and your oral presentation included in a single file.

Part 6

The last slide of your presentation should contain a slide called "References" and on this page you will write the APA formatted reference for the article you have covered.

APA citations are written in a specific format depending on the type of resource. You will need to utilize the APA Manual that you had to purchase to take this class to find out how to format your reference.

Criteria for Success

Use the rubric below as a guide to this assignment.

Slide Show Format   10 points

Presentation is in PowerPoint or Keynote format.

Article Structure   30 points

The slide show covers each of the major components of the article's structure.

Reference   10 points

The last slide contains the APA formatted reference for the article.

Narration   30 points

The slide show contains an embedded oral presentation that can be played along with each slide.

Mechanics   20 points

Spelling, syntax, and organizational structure of the presentation. Slides are aesthetically pleasing.

More on Writing

Attention

Credit, where Credit is Due

In the last Chapter you were briefly introduced to a bit of what is called APA format. In the assignment you did, you had to format your article in APA format.

In this Chapter we are going to focus more on the expectation to not only cite your sources in APA format but to use the Concise Guide to APA Style to influence and shape all of your professional writing.

First, however, you are going to learn about finding your voice....your Academic Voice.

Luckily, you won't have to get a Prince to kiss you to get it back before sundown!

Ariel trades her voice for legs and can only get it back when she gets Erik to kiss her.

The Little Mermaid

Learning Outcomes

Upon completion of this Chapter, students should be able to:

1. Discuss the concept of Academic Voice.

2. Utilize the Concise Guide to APA Style to identity formatting rules for writing undergraduate level papers.

3. Identify resources for applying APA style within MS Word.

Teaching

Academic Voice

Throughout your schooling you have had a variety of opportunities to express your knowledge of topics, your evaluation of problems, and the products of your critical thinking. Each of these represent experiences important in the career-spanning process of developing your own **academic voice**.

While there are many avenues for the development of academic voice, we mostly recognize this construct in writing. An author's **voice** is their unique way of writing and telling stories. You may have a favorite author who writes things in a very specific way that you can recognize immediately.

One of my favorite fiction authors is Dean Koontz. I have read nearly every one of his books and as soon as I start reading one I have to smile as his writing is immediately apparent.

Dean Koontz

Academic voice is similar to the type of voice that I recognize in Koontz' writing, but it also rests in an environment of reference to other authors and ideas. Ideas are not presented alone, they are presented in context of the related work of other people.

Culture and Academic Voice

Culture is the term that describes all the norms, values, and expectations of a particular group. We are **socialized** in our culture through institutions such as school, family, religion, and the economy. Academic voice is contextual to the field of study that it is being exercised in. Biologist have a culture regarding their academic voice that is different that those in psychology.

Early in your college career you begin developing your academic voice largely through reading the work of others and writing papers, essays, discussion posts, presentations, and oral discussions. You have even been asked to evaluate information and form your own conclusions about that information.

One of the key aspects of the culture of psychology rests in learning the norms and expectations in writing commonly referred to as APA style. APA stands for the American Psychological Association and the "style" is a set of language, writing, and presentation rules that set the bar for "professional writing" in the field.

It is important to recognize a some facts about APA style:

- The style outlined in official resources by the APA is largely targeted at professionals who wish to submit manuscripts for publication in one of their many journals. It can be said that the entirety of the rules actually only apply when submitting professional work for publication.

- Many other branches of academics have adopted the style as their own. You may encounter biologists, sociologists, philosophers, and many other professions using the APA style guides for their own writing.

- Many academics are not clear about the extent to which they expect student writing to comply with APA style. Some may simply require a title page and APA style references while others want papers written with much more stringent adherence to other rules of writing such as in-text citations, tables, and essay formation.

- Students are sometimes asked to write in a context that is counter-intuitive to the application of APA style. Online discussion posts and essay questions are not the target of the APA style rules and they are often difficult to apply completely in these situations.

A Manual for Students

Certainly not in response to my requests to the APA for clarification on these points, the APA has published a manual specific to the needs of students. Application of these rules can still be challenging but the new manual serves a very important role in the development of academic voice while still a student. As discussed in the previous Chapter, here is the Concise Guide to APA Style.

Concise Guide to APA Style (7th Ed.)
The Official APA Style Guide for Students

Getting to Know the Guide

This is not a novel, it has no gripping plot line or characters, it is a tool. The guide is a reference tool for you to look up the rules related to writing and communicating this aspect of the culture of your academic voice.

While we often use the guide to simply look up how to do a citation, it is valuable to spend time in the first three chapters.

1. Student Paper Types, Elements, and Format

2. Writing Style and Grammar

3. Bias Free Language Guidelines

This part actually makes for some interesting reading about how to shape your academic voice early in your career.

The next three chapters take on details related to formatting sentences and other elements of your paper.

4. Punctuation, Lists, and Italics

5. Spelling, Capitalization, and Abbreviation.

Since we are often writing material that is supported by quantitative data (numbers) and we often wish to summarize this data into tables and graphs, the next two chapters discuss these guidelines.

6. Numbers and Statistics

7. Tables and Figures

As students, you are often asked to write about the work of others. Even when you are asked to draw your own conclusions, you must provide supporting evidence and data from other authors. You accomplish this by giving credit to others' knowledge as you write about it. You then provide a way for your readers to look up these original sources themselves.

8. Works Credited in Text

9. References List

The manual ends with a chapter full of examples of different types of sources you may encounter. In the modern world where a lot of information is published online and in digital formats, the formatting of references to the works is continually challenging.

10. Reference Examples

Also, don't neglect the fact that the book also has an Index. The index sorts all the important terms in the book and provides you with the page or pages where these terms are used. This is an incredible useful way of using the book and getting right to the section that you need.

MS Word and APA Style

Microsoft Word is a powerful word processor that enables you to format all aspects of your document into APA Style. Some of these processes are automated but many of them require that you become pretty skilled at using Microsoft Word!

I've included a great video that explain how to format your paper in APA Style using MS Word. This video

APA Format in Word 2016
In 4 Minutes

APA Format in MS Word

portrays MS Word 2016 for Windows so there may be some differences between your version of Word, but the principles are all the same.

APA Format Tables

We often have to display data in the form of data tables and APA Style dictates how these tables should be formatted.

Here is an example from a very important study!

Table 1
Wood the Woodchucks Chucked in Experiment 1

Woodchuck	Wood chucked (in kg)	%
1	423.9	94.2
2	373.0	82.9
4	347.0	77.1
6	411.3	91.4

Note. Each virtual woodchuck received a 450-kg woodpile. Woodchucks 3 and 5 were removed from the analysis because they would not chuck wood.

The details of each element of this table form are outlined in the Concise Guide to APA Style.

I've included a video that explains how to use the formatting tools in MS Word to build a table like this one.

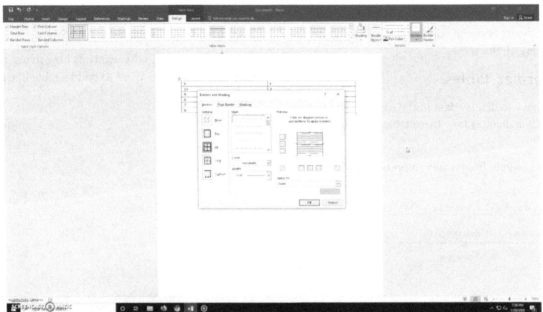

Formatting and APA Style table in MS Word

Assessment

Chapter 6 Discussion - Bias

In general people have a lot of blind spots and biases in their thinking. As we become scientists and apply our reasoning skills in a scientific manner we become better at avoiding these biases in our work. They are always there, scientists are first and foremost, humans. But they are less common.

Discuss how the practice of continual reference to external data to justify your own thinking and conclusions serve as a method for reducing cognitive blind spots and bias in your writing?

Chapter 6 Quiz - Scavenger Hunt

Using the Concise Guide to APA Style, state the page number (just the number, just the first page it it answers across a number of pages) where you can answer the following questions. If you wisely use the index, you can find these quickly, but take the time to go to the page and review that section, the more you familiarize yourself with the nuances of this style, the better you will be at writing this way.

1. Where would I find the list of elements of a title page?

2. How far, in inches, do you have to indent the first line in every paragraph (express your answer in decimals, such as 1.4)?

3. On what page do we find information about numbers expressed in words?

4. On what page will you find the start the section on plagiarism?

5. On what page will you find the start of the section on in-text citations?

6. If the article you are referencing has more than two authors, on what page would you find information about how many of the names to include within the in-text citation?

7. On what page will you find the APA principles on the use of direct quotations?

8. When creating your references list, what page provides information on the citation of articles from a database or archive (like EBSCO)?

9. On what page can you find information on the format and order of references?

10. On what page can you find information about the use of abbreviations in the references list?

Academic Planning

7

Attention

Academic Paths

Many of you will be at the very beginning of your study of psychology. At this point you may have some very specific career goals but this is the time to do some curious exploration of the broad range of concepts, ideas, and focal points of psychology by carefully selecting your elective courses on topics will expand you thoughts about psychology.

As we engage in long-term planning you will be able to take a look at the small selection that KVCC offers. You might even take a look at the fascinating classes offered by other institutions which will open up you mind!

Learning Outcomes

Upon completion of this Chapter, students should be able to:

1. Review your curriculum requirements for the program.

2. Enact your Student-Advisor Relationship Plan.

3. Register for courses in the next semester.

4. Establish a long term plan to complete your degree.

Teaching

Graduation Starts Now!

Maybe you have heard this saying before...

"He who fails to plan is planning to fail"
- Sir Winston Churchill

I'm going to assume that your goal is to graduate from this program! I'm also going to assume that some of you may have very specific plans about what you intend to do after graduation while some of you are floating on the waters of knowledge and waiting to ride a wave of inspiration, should it come along.

I'm good with either of these!

In this Chapter we are going to explore the resources you need to plan how you are going to graduate in a timely and cost-effective manner. We are also going to take the opportunity to access the wisdom of your Academic Advisor to discuss your future!

We might not be able to entirely predict your future, but we can at least come to some conclusions as to what you PLAN to be doing both here at KVCC and beyond!

The Limits of Planning

At the beginning of Spring 2020 I had a number of very interesting in-class activities planned out for my classes. I worked on them quite a bit because I'm not really an "activity" kind of teacher...I like to talk a lot.

Well we all know what happened next...

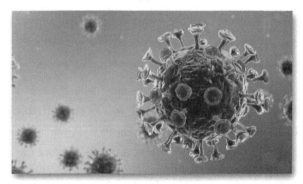

So...all the best intentions and planning were disrupted by COVID-19. However, as with many of my colleagues, we were not wrecked by this. We pivoted. We responded quickly in moving material online and reworking activities and policies to convert to online delivery. It was not perfect, but for many it worked. We even learned that some of it was better and we now have some "new normals".

I tell this story to make the point that planning is great, but you have to be flexible for if and when circumstances change. Personally, I was ready for COVID because I had designed all my classes for online delivery already, I simply had to add the online discussions to my face-to-face classes and we were "off to the races".

The second part of planning is planning for changes or chances that might come along. We can do both. You might have to deal with disappointments when it comes to changing plans, but if you work this out before the changes happen, you will do just fine. Any number of things can come along and cause you to change. Some of the possible impacts on YOU are as follows.

- It might take you longer to finish.

- You may end up retaking a class.

- You might find your interests and your goals changing.

- You might have to take online classes.

- You might have to take a face-to-face class.

- You might not get into the class you want to take and have to choose another.

- You might find you don't like to study Psychology and change your major.

- You might have to take some time off.

- New and different opportunities may appear.

You can ready yourself for these kinds of changes by acknowledging that circumstances beyond your control may enter in and upset your plan.

If this happens, you have an advisor and other supports to help you through the challenge. We will explore these concepts more in the next chapter on Career Planning.

Assessment

Chapter 7 Assignment - Planning

Purpose

The assignment for this Chapter focuses developing a short- and long-range plan for completing your Psychology degree at KVCC.

Skills and Knowledge

You will demonstrate the following skills and knowledge by completing this assignment:

1. Identify web-based sources for information on the curriculum for the Associates of Science in Psychology.

2. Identify web-based sources for information on the courses offered in the next semester.

3. Register for courses for the next semester.

4. Develop a long-range plan to complete the degree in line with expectations for work or continuing education after graduation.

Task

Your advisor has developed an Advising Guide to be used to document your plan to complete all the academic requirements for the degree. The document is in MS Word format and includes information in the required courses, elective courses, and general education requirements for graduation.

This assignment will occur in a number of steps.

Step 1 - Planning next Semester

1. Review the Advising Guide to document courses you have completed.

2. Review the curriculum expectations as they are presented in the Psychology program website.

3. Access the list of courses that are being offered in the next semester.

4. Develop a list of the courses you plan to sign up for in the next semester.

Step 2 - Consider After Graduation

This may be a challenging part of this assignment. I want you to consider what you plan on doing next semester. Most students choose to go on to another college to pursue a Bachelors Degree in Psychology or a related field. Some choose to stay at KVCC and get another Associates Degree.

If you plan on going on to complete your Bachelors Degree at another college, you are to engage in the following steps:

1. Review the program of choice on the website of the college.

2. Document the contact information for the program you are interested in.

3. Match the expectations of the program with the expectations and course options within the degree at KVCC.

4. Identify classes you wish to take at KVCC that match the requirements at the other school.

5. Reach out and make initial contact with the program at the other school.

6. Potentially seek advice from that school as to which courses you should complete at KVCC to maximize your transfer to that school.

Part 3 - Meet with your Advisor

Meet with your advisor in order to fully complete the Advising Guide document and plan out both next semester and your plan for graduation.

Part 4 - Write a brief paper describing your plan

You will submit a paper that includes all the elements described in the rubric below. You will not need to submit your actual Advising Guide document.

Criteria for Success

Use the rubric below as a guide to this assignment.

Title page   10 points
Includes the name of the assignment, class, your name, and date.

Dream   20 points
Write a paragraph outlining your current dream regarding your career and how this degree fits in.

After Graduation   50 points
Outline your plans for after graduation. This should include any number of options you may consider, contact information for those options, and initial plans to sign up for classes in the Psychology program that align with these goals.

Mechanics   20 points
Spelling, syntax, and organizational structure of the paper. Clear and organized.

Career Planning

Attention

Serendipity

The word refers to something positive that happens by chance. Like when we run into an old friend we have not seen for a long time in an unexpected place. Or when we find a dollar bill on the ground. We can all probably list a lot of instances in our own life when this has happened.

There is also a theory of serendipity related to career development, it is called **Planned Happenstance**. This theory arose from data that indicated that many people in very satisfying careers did not necessarily plan to be in those careers. Often they were in the "right place at the right time" and the chanced upon an opportunity.

While this Chapter is all about planning to achieve your goals, you can also plan to be ready for those chance encounters that could change your life. You can plan for happenstance (chance events) and enable yourself to be flexible when the time comes!

MOVIE - Krumboltz Theory of Career Development and Happenstance Theory

Learning Outcomes

Upon completion of this Chapter, students should be able to:

1. Utilize online resources to explore potential careers in Psychology.

2. Identify the credentials you need to obtain to aspire to these careers.

3. Identify a long-term Education and Career Plan.

Teaching

Letters (after your name)

Many jobs within our economy require specific **skills** and **credentials**. A common way for a person to identify their credentials is to include them in their name on official documents, often in the form of a sequence of letters that indicate a certificate, license, status, or degree. I'll use my own name to provide some examples.

Mark H. Kavanaugh, MS

Indicates I have a Masters of Science

Mark H. Kavanaugh, Ph.D.

Indicates I have a Doctorate

Mark H. Kavanaugh, MHRT/C

Indicates I have a Certificate

Dr. Mark H. Kavanaugh

Indicates I'm a Doctor

Other examples include "RN", "MD", "MSN", "LSW", "MCSW", "LCPC", etc.

Cultural Expectations

These indications are important for our society to work. If you are in the hospital and someone comes in to give you a shot, you are going to look for the letters after their name to be sure that they are qualified to give you the shot!

The regulations for credentialing and the accreditation requirements for school programs (like those at KVCC) work together to assure that the individual who has specific letters can be relied upon to "know their stuff".

Jobs and Letters

As you explore your particular career path you will find that specific kinds of work will require specific kinds of credentials. The use of terms like "Physician", "Nurse", and "Psychologist" are often tied to these credentials and those without those credentials cannot call themselves by the names.

One of the most popular ways we gain credentials is to go to school (in the form of training and academic classes.)

The Scholastic Pathway

The **Associates of Science in Psychology** is just the beginning of a diverse pathway toward achieving the credentials and skills you need to do the work you want to do.

What can I do with this?

There are only three real outcomes of getting an associates degree in psychology.

- To get a job that asks for the skills you have learned.

- To explore the world of psychology.

- To prepare yourself to go on to other, higher degrees in psychology or related fields.

Skills and Exploration

As we will see in the next Chapter on Outcomes Assessment, this degree will help you explore the knowledge base of the field and help you develop specific skills that are applicable in nearly every aspect of your life. Sometimes it is really a matter of how you present these skills on your resume or to a potential employer.

One skill that you are going to learn in this program is how to find and read academic, peer reviewed literature. You might, at first, list this skill on your resume as:

I can locate articles on a topic in EBSCO

This is an accurate assessment of that skill, but there may be some more compelling and attractive ways to write it:

I can utilize academic databases to evaluate peer-reviewed literature to explore solutions to problems.

This is the same skill, but it is much more easily applied to a variety of situations (and it sounds cool).

We will return to this type of thinking in the next Chapter!

Higher Degrees in Psychology

Many of you will want to start thinking about the next steps in your scholastic career. You will want to explore different career paths (jobs) and discover what credentials you need and then determine how you are going to get those credentials!

Even if you are just here for skills and exploration, I'm going to ask you to take a look at possible careers in psychology and related fields.

Psi Beta Resources

Psi Beta is the honors society for students with an interest in psychology attending community colleges. There is only one Psi Beta Chapter in Maine...right here at KVCC! You will want to explore the benefits of membership and strive for that level of excellence!

For this Chapter, we are going to utilize some of the free resources that are available on the Psi Beta website concerning career development.

Professional Development / Career Readiness Resources for Psi Beta Members

Let me point out some of the resources I recommend as you explore this site:

Zoom Presentation on Careers

Watch this presentation and download the PowerPoint slides. (The movie itself has the slides but the graphics are really small.)

This is a great overview of the credentialing options within the field of psychology.

Online Career-Exploration Resource for Psychology Majors

This link is to an interactive MS Word file that will allow you to explore all sorts of different careers in psychology based on the following general categories:

- Business, Advertising, and Finance
- Children and Families
- Counseling
- Education

- Health and Medical Services

- Human Resources

- Law and Law Enforcement

- Military

- Psychology

- Religion and Spirituality

- Social and Human Services

- Sports, Fitness, and Recreation

- Technology

- Therapy

- Other

This document provides links to official sites about different careers, career descriptions, pay, job growth potentials, and academic programs.

Assessment

Chapter 8 Discussion A - Chance

In the Attention section you encountered the notion of Planned Happenstance. Share any stories you may have about chance encounters and experiences you may have had. They can be huge life-changing ones or small and amazing ones!

Chapter 8 Discussion B - Career

Engage with the Psi Beta resources that I have in clued (in particular, the video and the career resources). Explore a number of different pathways. Include pathways Different from the one(s) you might have your mind set on.

Share the experience of your journey and some of the possible career paths you might explore!

Outcomes Assessment

9

Attention

What does a Degree Mean?

With tuition prices and student loans so high across the country (not so much the case at community colleges) the perceived value of a college degree is being questioned. If you are going to spend money, add stress to your life, and do "fun" things like writing papers, taking tests, doing presentations, and serving in your community...you might want to know what you are supposed to get out of it!

KVCC Accreditation with NECHE

In the complex social structure of our society, you want to be sure that you are getting what you pay for. KVCC is a publicly funded institution (your taxes pay a lot of the cost of running KVCC), so we are responsible to the

State of Maine to assure we are doing what we are supposed to do. NECHA is an organization that evaluates the effectiveness of KVCC on meeting its missions as a business and as a school. This accreditation body holds the college to standards of quality and consistency outlined in their accreditation guidelines.

NECHE Standards for Accreditation

The KVCC Mission

As an institution, KVCC has a mission statement that guides our processes and decision making.

Kennebec Valley Community College prepares students to achieve their educational, professional, and personal goals in a supportive environment through shared values of responsibility, integrity and respect.

The combination of the standards from NECHE and KVCC's own mission and values, rest assured that we are continually evaluating how well we do what we do.

The Value of a Degree

We are still left with the question, what is the value of getting a college degree. Well, there are lots of ways to measure value, and many of them are enhanced by a college education:

- **More Money** - Persons with a college degree will, on average, earn much more money of their careers.

- **Specific Jobs Require It** - You can't become a doctor with out a degree (many of them) and other jobs are similar.

- **Understanding** - A well balanced, liberal-arts education will provide you with opportunities to understand how our world works.

- **Work Skills** - Regardless of what you do after you graduate, you will be in possession of marketable skills transferable to any job.

- **Perspective** - Another advantage of a liberal-arts education is the enhanced ability to see things from multiple perspectives. This leads to civility and respect for individual differences.

- **Grace under Pressure** - You develop the skills to perform under pressure.

- **More Ideological Independence** - You are less likely to be impacted by political rhetoric, unlikely stories, and bias; making you a better and more thoughtful citizen and voter.

- **Advantageous Knowledge** - You will be exposed to information that you can use to get ahead, complete more successfully, and fulfill your goals.

- **Respect** - A college degree carries respect and honor among many people.

Is it worth it…?

Well, I'm biased, I have been involved in education for nearly my entire life and I have a lot of degrees. My answer is a resounding YES!

Program Specific Outcomes

In addition to the generic outcomes I just listed that apply to any degree, this Chapter is going to focus on the outcomes of your learning in the Associates of Science in Psychology.

This program is based largely on two separate sets of guidelines: The American Psychological Association (APA) Guidelines for the Undergraduate Psychology Major and the American Association of Colleges and Universities (AAC&U) Value Added Learning for Undergraduate Education (VALUE) guidelines.

Learning Outcomes

Upon completion of this Chapter, students should be able to:

1. Identify and discuss the mapping of APA Learning Outcomes in the Associates of Science in Psychology degree program.

2. Identify and discuss the mapping of AAC&U VALUE Outcomes in the Associates of Science in Psychology degree program.

Teaching

Mapping Outcomes

Maps show you were things are. You all likely have a map app on your device and you can find nearly anything!

If this program says you are learning specific knowledge and skills, the map of these outcomes is used to find where those experiences are. Actually, the map show you the activities that you need to engage in (discussions, quizzes, assignments, etc.) to DEMONSTRATE that you have attained a learning outcome. For the purpose of evaluation, we refer to these activities collectively as **assessments**. Assessments are not only used to determine what you have learned and to determine your grade, they are used to evaluate the effectiveness of the course and the teacher.

When we map these across all the classes in the program we have a fairly complex picture of the things you will need to do to demonstrate these skills.

CourseBooks

As you learned about earlier, I have written most of the CourseBooks for this program and I have edited all of them. In each CourseBook you are going to find a section at the beginning of the book that provides the map for program learning outcomes in that specific course. It's the section titled **Outcome Alignment** and you can see that there are two parts to this....one identifies the assessments that align with the VALUE outcomes and the other identifies the assessments that align with the APA outcomes. This is one of the main reasons I developed the CourseBook model of content delivery. It allowed me to outlines these alignments for each course and keep them consistent regardless of who is teaching the class!

APA and VALUE Outcomes

If you look at the first section of this CourseBook you will find an outline of all the APA and VALUE outcomes. As you look through these outcomes you will notice that I note specific assessments that I believe align with the outcome. This tells you that the specific assessment has something to do with that outcome.

All the assessments in a course are SOMEWHERE in this list.

Some of them are in red.

These assessments are the ones I use to do course and program evaluation.

You will also notice that not all the outcomes are covered in the class. That is OK...they are covered multiple times across all the classes in the program!

Assessment

Chapter 9 Discussion - Outcomes

Examine the alignment of outcomes in this CourseBook and any other CourseBook you may have. Discuss your experience with some of these assignments and how confident they make you feel about those particular outcomes.

It is OK to critique my work as well! If you find that a specific assignment does not really align well, point it out!

Self-Assessment

10

Attention

Adaptation

COVID-19 brought on a number of challenges. Aside from the illness and death, the pandemic continues to change the way we do things. Many were called upon to adapt their usual routines. Change, of course, nearly always brings about a certain amount of stress. One of the most important traits that we possess is a combination of skills and intelligence that allow us to **adapt** to different situations.

Leon C. Megginson

"It is not the strongest of the species that survives, nor the most intelligent. It is the one most adaptable to change."

You might think that a quote like this arose from Charles Darwin himself, but it was actually from Leon C. Megginson. It also had to do a lot more with leadership in organizations going through change than it had to do with a pandemic! That value of this statement is powerful none-the-less.

We will examine what I think is the specific skill set needed to maximize adaptation to changing circumstances. Keep in mind that other aspects of our lives change rapidly as well. Technology, economy, safety and security, global politics, etc.

Learning Outcomes

Upon completion of this Chapter, students should be able to:

1. Discuss the experience of this class.

2. Assess personal 21st Century Skills.

3. Assess personal Non-Academic Skills

4. Write a Skill Development Plan.

Teaching

The Modern Workplace

Technology is changing the workplace very quickly. One statistic that I heard of is very telling. If you were going to provide guidance to students who are currently Freshman in high school as to career they will have available to them after 4 years of college (a total of 8 years) approximately 80% of the available jobs don't exist yet! They will come about because of changes that occurred during that 8 year period!

So what do you need to have NOW in order to survive and thrive in a quickly changing work environment?

Programs like Psychology

You have likely discovered (or you already knew) that getting an Associates in Science in Psychology does not lead to related position in the world of Psychology. At least there are not many. This is not the same as a degree in Nursing or Accounting.

The strength of the program however, is in how it addresses 21st Century Skills.

21st Century Skills

This set of skills comes out of research conducted asking business leaders and managers what they are looking for. These leaders and managers are looking for individuals who will be able to adapt to the changes they anticipate will come over time. These skills exist in three categories:

Learning skills (the four C's) teaches students about the mental processes required to adapt and improve upon a modern work environment.

Literacy skills (IMT) focuses on how students can discern facts, publishing outlets, and the technology behind them. There's a strong focus on determining trustworthy sources and factual information to separate it from the misinformation that floods the Internet.

Life skills (FLIPS) take a look at intangible elements of a student's everyday life. These intangibles focus on both personal and professional qualities.

Evidence of 21st Century Skills

Understanding that your future employer is going to want these kinds of skills, how would you go about documenting them? On the next page you will see some graphic representations of these skills and a link to a comprehensive website to explore each of these.

You may also notice some overlap between these skills and those outlined in the VALUE outcomes from the previous Chapter.

Non-cognitive Skills

Visit this site to learn all about 21st Century Skills and why they are Important

As a psychologist, it is nonsense for me to consider that there are skills that do not involve our cognition, but I was not in charge of naming these particular skills! They do, however, involve your personality.

In the field of psychology there are a number of constructs that are both challenging to define and create debate on the nature vs nurture development questions. These are **personality** and **intelligence**.

You will learn about these particular areas in detail as you make your way through the program. For now, non-cognitive skills have a lot of similarity to personality traits. Are we born with these traits or do we develop them through experience (learning)?

The answer to the nature/nurture question is nearly always "both". As we examine these skills/traits consider that for some these come easy because they are "wired" for them. For others, some work can be done to create these traits in your own personality.

Developing these skills requires a high degree of internal reflection on your own personality.

Social and Emotional Skills

In a world in which we are increasingly isolated by computers, cell phones, and television, we need to continuously learn how to interact with one another. We need to know how to treat each other, and how to address each other's needs. If our social behavior is left unchecked, it could lead to multiple problems down the road.

Social and Emotional Health can be described using the following model.

Character

Social-Emotional Health Model

Emotional Competence

Emotion Regulation

Empathy

Self-Control

Belief-in-Self

Self-Efficacy

Persistence

Self-Awareness

Engaged Living

Optimism

Zest

Gratitude

Belief-in-Others

Family Coherence

Peer Support

School Support

Building character is definitely nothing new to the 21st century. However, it's still an incredibly important non-academic skill to focus on in modern day society. We must possess self-control, especially in an age in which so many stimuli are at our fingertips. We also must foster a sense of curiosity about the world around and; and not in a superficial, "Let's Google it" manner. We must yearn to explore the world, and find answers for ourselves rather than relying on a machine to give us everything. We should also build up our confidence, so we are optimistic about our lives, so we can face the world knowing we can improve it in some way.

Growth Mindset

W are constantly growing and learning. We should be constantly conscious of the fact that each experience we go through is a chance to learn something even in a non-academic setting. This will help us make the most out of bad situations, because we'll always be looking at what we learned, rather than the fact that we messed up (or something was messed up). We must learn to be okay with messing up and how to learn from our mistakes. When we stop learning, that's when trouble starts to pile up. As Noah Webster (of Webster's dictionary) once said, "The virtues of men are of more consequence to society than their abilities…for this reason, the heart should be cultivated."

Metacognition

These are the non-academic skills that we use in order to know which other skills to use. We need to have the ability to assess a situation and determine the skillset we need to bring to it, what we need to learn, and when to ask for help. It's important to focus not just on what skills to learn, but *how* to use them as well. Sometimes the development of these traits occurs in the typical problem-solving that goes along in regular life.

Grit

Life isn't easy. The sooner we figure that out, the better off we'll be. We ned to learn that it's totally okay to fail, as long as we pick ourselves up and keep pushing until we succeed. We also need to understand the difference between passing by the skin of their teeth and passing with flying colors. One will earn us just enough to get by in life, but the other will allow us to truly get ahead. Being rigorous in all activities, and putting our all into everything we set out to do, is of utmost importance if we want to live their life to the fullest. Even something simple like asking ourselves, "What did I fail at today?" allows us to gain insight and reflect that failure happens everyday but can be overcome with persistence or through another avenue.

Soft Skills

This last set of non-academic skills is a bit of a misnomer. Any skill you can learn is important, so calling these skills "soft" makes them seem less so. However, now more than ever it is important that we learn the basics of professionalism. We need to know it's important to be punctual, and to dress properly. We need to exhibit good manners and align social conventions, not just during our working hours, but at all times. It's increasingly important that we understand that their online persona will allow others to judge our real-life personality, so it's important to be prudent both on and offline. If we don't pay attention to these social conventions, all other skills we learn will ultimately be null and void.

Assessment

Chapter 10 Discussion - Class

In this discussion I would like you to reflect on the experience of this class. What did you get out of it? What could be improved? Share your next steps in your journey as well.

Chapter 10 Assignment - Self

Purpose

The purpose of this assignment is to assess the current status of your 21st Century and Non-cognitive skills. These are essential skills to develop in nearly every facet of life, not just work. In addition, you will also develop a plan to address areas of weakness in these skills.

This is a rather in-depth assignment with a lot of skills to assess and develop. My goals are for you to be aware of these skills and their importance. However, it is beneficial for you to really take the time to do this assignment. This is much more about your personal growth and development than just doing an assignment to pass a class.

Skills and Knowledge

You will demonstrate the following skills and knowledge by completing this assignment:

1. Assess personal proficiency in 21st Century Skills

2. Assess personal proficiency in Non-cognitive skills.

3. Develop a comprehensive plan to address any deficiencies.

Task

This is a rather methodical type of paper. For each of the 21st Century and Non-cognitive skill areas you will document the following:

- Name of Skill (in bold)

- Paragraph analyzing your current level of this skill with example(s).

- Paragraph outlining SPECIFIC steps you can take to enhance this skill. If you have proficiency in a skill, then outline how you are going to PRACTICE this skill.

It is vital that the plans for enhancing and/or practicing are very SPECIFIC and written as action items.

Criteria for Success

Use the rubric below as a guide to this assignment.

Title page   10 points

Includes the name of the assignment, class, your name, and date.

Skill Assessment   70 points

All the 21st Century and Non-cognitive skills are assessed with a plan of action to develop and/or practice.

Mechanics   20 points

Spelling, syntax, and organizational structure of the paper. Clear and organized.

Special Assignments

Enlightenment Now

Purpose

The purpose of this assignment is to explore the ideas in Steven Pinker's famous title, *Enlightenment Now*.

Skills and Knowledge

You will demonstrate the following skills and knowledge by completing this assignment:

1. Reading and reflecting on the role of reason, science, and humanism in the modern world.

2. Apply this knowledge to develop a personal mindset for the study of psychology.

Task

In many of the courses you will take in this program you will encounter a section titled "Special Assignments." The tasks contained in this section are broader in scope, take longer to complete, and are more "project-like." For this course I have a very special reading assignment, and we are going to discuss aspects of this book through the class.

Enlightenment Now : The Case for Reason, Science, Humanism, and Progress

by Steven Pinker

Available online and at our Campus Store

Throughout the course you will be asked to read specific chapters in the book and participate in discussions and activities related to that content.

The grading for the discussions and activities will be the same as regular online discussions.

We will not be discussing every aspect or chapter in the book but it is highly advisable that you read the entire thing. Personally, I found this to be one of the most important books I have ever encountered.

What follows are the chapter and descriptions of the Graded Discussions and activities created in this class. Please review the online materials for due dates.

Part I - Introduction

Our first module with our special reading assignment introduces you to Steven Pinker (our author) and his major thesis.

The links below provide you with information about our author to consume while you are reading the first three chapters in the book *Enlightenment Now: A Case for Reason, Science, Humanism, and Progress.*

Expectations for this module include the following:

- Review the online biography of Dr. Steven Pinker.

- Watch the Enlightenment Now video.

- Read Chapters 1-3 in the book (pages 7-35)

- Participate in the graded discussion (you are required to create at least one post in response to the prompt and reply to at least two others' prompts for full credit.)

About Steven Pinker

Enlightenment Now

Part I Discussion

The first three chapters of our book introduce the notion of the term **enlightenment** as both a way of thinking and as representative of a particular age in western history. Pinker highlights the importance of the **Scientific Revolution** and human **Reason** as examples of human excellence despite the presence of overwhelming **Counter-Enlightenment** ideas in our world. Discuss the importance of these concepts, the challenges you personally face in them, and examples of these phenomena from your own life.

Part II - Progress

In this section we are going to take on both **progress** and the fear of progress (**progress phobia**) as Pinker calls it.

Reading for this discussion includes:

- Chapter 4 - Progress Phobia
- Chapter 5 - Life
- Chapter 6 - Health
- Chapter 7 - Sustenance
- Chapter 8 - Wealth

The picture that Pinker paints in these Chapters is startling considering what we hear on the news. The news is not FAKE, it is SELECTIVE. The bigger picture is that we are doing remarkably well in each of these areas and amazing progress has been made.

Taking the quiz for the Progress discussion may earn you one of these bad boys!

Part II Discussion A

Pinker examines a number of players in the world that benefit from the perception that progress is the problem rather than the solution. Speculate and discuss who may be the winners in a world that thinks it is going to "hell"?

Part II Discussion B

Pinker presents amazing data on progress in the world. The fear is that backward thinking, good 'ol days, and sheer ignorance may push back against the positive progress we have made.

In the book we are introduced to the **Ignorance Project** which strives to create a "fact-based worldview". The assessments that they have used have demonstrated that the general population is misguided in many ways about the facts of the world. Let's see how you do on this!

Take the Gapminder test and report any surprises. Give this test to your friends, family, etc. Report out what happens. Share summaries of the information brought to light across Chapters 5, 6, 7, and 8.

Gapminder Test

Part III - Inequality and Fairness

In this section we are discussing a core concept that lays at the foundation of much of the social sciences...inequality.

Read Chapter 9 in Pinker's book.

Take note of the comparison he makes between inequality and fairness. We are often OK with inequality as long as it is fair.

Next Pinker explores the trends of inequality both in the US and in the world. The take away is that government programs like taxes and other redistributions, investment in education and infrastructure, and economic growth have increased the degree of basic inequality but have also raised the standard of living for all levels of society. We stand on the brink of abolition of absolute poverty, and in the section on the "stuff" that the poor have (as compared to the rich of a century ago) makes clear that we are all really doing a lot better.

Problems continue. Absolute poverty exists, unfair politics and policies exist, and we are faced with an increased presence of the desire to return to a false reality of the 1950s "good ol' days" which were not as good as we remember them.

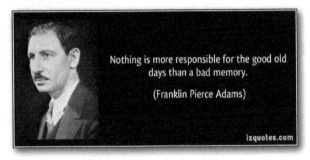

Nothing is more responsible for the good old days than a bad memory.

(Franklin Pierce Adams)

izquotes.com

For our discussion, I want us to contemplate two topics, one is the concept of inequality vs fairness and the other is the inaccurate memories that remember a golden past that was simply non-existent for many more people than than today.

Part III Discussion

Consider your notions of inequality and fairness. This can be expressed in terms of the global inequity or very personal on the soccer field. Why do we sometimes envy those who are successful when they have achieved their status fairly? How do are perceptions of how fair it happened shape our perceptions of the inequity?

In addition, consider the notion of the "Golden Years". Our writer provides compelling arguments that the most assured contributor to the concept of a glorified past is a bad memory. Reflect on this on how this philosophy is rising in the current political establishment.

Part IV - Bayesian Reasoning

Pinker has continually alluded to the concept of reason. The Enlightenment itself is often referred to as the Age of Reason. In Chapter 21 we are introduced to a specific method of applying human reasoning. Bayesian Reasoning is the process by which we content with an issue by understanding the probability of and taking into account all the causal factors that we know are related to the issue. Pinker relates that the individuals who were the best at "predicting" the future used this method rather than generic ideas and principles.

The principle at work is that events are caused by many small factors all contributing their individual influence to the outcome. This is messy and complex. But, it allows us to escape the cognitive traps of bias and availability heuristics.

This counters the proposition of extreme solutions. Hot topics such as abortion, gun control, welfare, and government/corporate spending each have extremist positions that are not even close to real solutions. The "devil is in the details" of messy, gray areas of solutions.

In this discussion, attempt to take on a social issue and approach it dispassionately in an effort to arrive at the gray solution. Help each other too.

Part IV Discussion

In this discussion, attempt to take on a social issue and approach it dispassionately in an effort to arrive at the gray solution. Help each other too.

Part V - Intelligibility vs Reductionism

Early childhood symbolic reasoning skills lead to one of the most fascinating and wonderful periods of time in our lives, the age of imaginative play! That block of wood we are pushing through the sand is not a block of wood, it is a truck. That dress up game we are playing were we are cops and robbers has a surreal quality in the minds of children.

Truly, the period of time up until pre-adolescence is filled with imagination, creativity, and a sense that the entire world is magical, not just Disney theme parks!

As we move into higher order thinking skills, we begin to lose this sense of the world and all its imagined beings (Easter Bunny, Santa, the creature-under-the-bed, etc.) There is actually a term for this and it is aptly named due to the sense of loss that comes with it for both children and their parents.

The Death of Childhood

This is not to mean that we let go of all aspects of magical thinking, in fact, we desperately hold on to a lot of them. We still correlate events in a magical way through astrology, chance occurrences, and the addition of deeper meaning to otherwise random events. Things like having an accident because we are supposed to learn a lesson from it..."everything happens for a reason" type thinking.

Even religion itself is magical, or supernatural. Faith itself sets it somewhat apart from science since faith is "believe despite the lack of evidence" in many respects. When science turns its eyes to religion it clearly points out the lack of evidence for supernatural powers. Yet we still believe.

As sensitive as we are to the nuances of our beliefs, rational or not, we are attached to the magical and "unknowable" quality of the world. Science seeks to explain things and make them **intelligible**, but this is seen by some as **reductionism**.

It is important to understand that something can become intelligible without reducing it. In fact, in most areas of scientific exploration, finding facts about how things work often create even more questions! The more we know, the more we know how little we know! (Read that sentence really slowly!)

Pinker shares that this distinction is often used to downplay science and accuse it of ill deeds. particularly when it seeks to take on issues such as social behavior, morality, and even the spiritual experience. These have been the topic areas of fields like religion and philosophy and those gardens have high fences and locked gates.

Pinker states that we are not rational actors but "**moralistic actors**; ...guided by intuition about authority, tribe, and purity; are committed to sacred beliefs that express their identity; are are drive by conflicting inclinations toward revenge and reconciliation" (p. 407).

Science attempts to provide the opportunity to make these aspects of our lives intelligible. However, we may find cherished aspects of who we are on the wrong side of the hypothesis. This is what we will discuss.

Consider aspects of your life that define who you are and what you think and believe (pretty much the same thing!). Share aspects of yourself that you would be reluctant to put into a scientific study out of fear that your identity would be subject to falsification.

Share why these aspects of yourself are sacred and potential outcomes should they prove to be wrong or misguided.

Part VI - Humanism

In this last chapter, Pinker lays out the major philosophical foundation of science, humanism. Humanism has the goal of "maximizing human flourishing - life, health, happiness, freedom, knowledge, love, (and) richness of experience."

Visit the American Humanist Association

There are philosophical objections to humanism but Pinker satisfactorily confronts them. Two other areas of human experience also object to humanism and provide a more challenging opposition. More challenging not because they are based in reality, but because of the emotional strength they possess over the minds of adherents.

The tag line on the American Humanist Association is "good without a god". I think this should be more broadly stated as "good without a dogma" and by this we can encompass these two major challenges:

- Religion
- Romantic/heroic/tribal/authoritarian complex

These are areas of conversation and debate that are deeply dividing our country and challenging its humanistic origins.

Separation of Church and State

The First Amendment in the US Constitution stipulates two specific clauses, the "establishment clause" which precludes the government from creating or favoring one religion over the other, and the "Free Exercise Clause" which protects all religious viewpoints and expressions provided they do not result in violations of other laws.

Case-by-case court history makes evident that this is not always a simple set of rules to follow. It is also of concern to many individuals with deep convictions either for the existence of god or not.

Nationalism and Populism

As present in our current public debates is the growing sense of nationalism and populism. It is, however, important to define these accurately.

Nationalism - Identification with one's own nation and support for its interests, especially to the exclusion or detriment of other nations.

I would add that with this is a quest to return to the "good old days" and "originalist interpretation" of the constitution as evidenced by the Supreme Court.

Populism - A political approach that strives to appeal to ordinary people who feel that their concerns are disregarded by established elite groups.

Populism has also targeted specific groups such as doctors and scientists as enemies of freedom. We saw this in the controversies associated with the COVID-19 pandemic.

It is not difficult to see the utility of these particular viewpoints, but they are opposed to the concepts and goals of humanism.

Humanism has a universal approach to ALL human flourishing, not only those in our own country. Humanism also respects science and the role of experts and those with expertise in the process of decision making (though it is clear that Pinker does not feel that all decision making should be handed over to scientists!)

Discuss how nationalism and populism are experienced in the US right now. What is attractive about these movements? How have recent changes in society challenged what Pinker has said about the values of reason, science, humanism, and progress?

Made in the USA
Columbia, SC
13 August 2022

65263417R00091